RUM ACROSS THE BORDER

A York State Book

RUM ACROSS

Overton's Corners Border Station

THE BORDER

The Prohibition Era in Northern New York

ALLAN S. EVEREST

SYRACUSE UNIVERSITY PRESS

First published 1978

First Paperback Edition 1991
91 92 93 94 95 96 97 98 99   6 5 4 3 2 1

This book is published with the assistance of a grant from the John Ben
Snow Foundation.

ALLAN S. EVEREST, Professor Emeritus of History, State University of New
York at Plattsburgh, is the author of *Moses Hazen and the Canadian Refu-
gees in the American Revolution, Our North Country Heritage,* and *The War
of 1812 in the Champlain Valley.* He has also written articles for *New York
History* and *Vermont History.*

The paper used in this publication meets the minimum requirements of American National Standard for Information Sciences – Permanence of Paper for
Printed Library Materials, ANSI Z39.48-1984. ∞™

Library of Congress Cataloging in Publication Data

Everest, Allan Seymour.
  Rum across the border.

  (A York State book)
  1. Prohibition – New York (State) 2. Smuggling
– New York (State) I. Title.
HV5090.N7E9   364.1'33   78-13768
ISBN 0-8156-0152-2 (alk. paper)
0-8156-2547-2 (pbk.: alk. paper)

Manufactured in the United States of America

Contents

The Stories They Tell

Y EARS AGO I undertook the little chore of satisfying my curiosity about what Prohibition had meant along an international border. It took me no time at all to discover that this was a bigger and more interesting subject than I had expected. Consequently, I grabbed my pen and tape recorder and rushed off to learn more of the story.

I attempt here to describe life in the Prohibition era through the eyes of the participants. Over the last dozen years I have interviewed customs officers, border patrolmen, bootleggers, lawyers, and civilians of the era. Their recollections provide authenticity to an incredible period, and they make this book an oral history of the 1920s and early 1930s. A sense of urgency spurred my efforts because several of the people I interviewed have since died, and all who grew up during the Prohibition years are now at least in their sixties.

Personal reminiscences of events more than

forty years old are sometimes inexact or incomplete. I have consequently supplemented the interviews with accounts from the newspapers and magazines of the day. In this way I have been able to relate in sequence and in their entirety some events that were only hinted at in an interview.

I have concerned myself with only one segment of the U.S.–Canadian border—that part between New York and Quebec but adjacent to Lake Champlain. It is a microcosm of the whole border. It is pierced by a waterway, Lake Champlain, 135 miles in length and stretching almost halfway to New York City, and it served the rumrunners well. So did the Delaware and Hudson Railroad, whose Montreal–New York tracks enter the United States at Rouses Point, New York. Moreover, numerous highways come into New York State from Quebec, and only a few were then guarded by customs stations. On each side of the border lay a broad zone of woods, sparse settlement, and country roads which offered the bootlegger an ideal setting for the first leg of his journey.

Fifty miles north of the border was the metropolis of Montreal, headquarters for much of the smuggling. Twenty miles within the United States the small city of Plattsburgh emerged as an important depot for the liquor traffic because the railroad and several of the highways converged upon it. The "Rum Trail" from Rouses Point to Albany for the most part followed U.S. Highway 9 and, as its name suggests, was an important thoroughfare for smugglers serving the cities of central and southern New York. Except for the great distances, rumrunners found that the Champlain Valley possessed all the qualities, including a cooperative citizenry, which the successful operation of their business required.

My interviews were particularly enriched by the contributions of two people. Jack Ross, now the village historian of Rouses Point and then a customs officer at the same place, informed me of the atmosphere of the times and the organization of the law-enforcement agencies. He also provided most of the pictures in this book. Sam Racicot, former bootlegger and now a resident of Rouses Point, talked freely about his own experiences, introduced me to other bootleggers, and ably interviewed one of them for me.

I appreciate the extensive help I had from two unusually competent students who formerly attended the State University College in Plattsburgh. This book would have been long delayed without the work of James Barnett and Kathleen Sullivan in researching newspapers and transcribing tapes. Dr. Charles Morrissey, former editor of *Vermont History* and an authority on oral history, read the original manuscript and made invaluable suggestions for its improvement. I have also been generously assisted in this work by the State University of New York through a grant from its Research Foundation.

Plattsburgh, New York   Allan S. Everest
Summer 1978

RUM ACROSS THE BORDER

How It Came About

*We, the undersigned, recognizing the evils of drunk-
enness and resolved to check its alarming increase,
with consequent poverty, misery and crime among
our people, hereby pledge ourselves that we will not
get drunk more than four times a year, viz., Fourth
of July, Muster Day, Christmas Day and Sheep
Shearing.*

Temperance pledge c. 1813

EVIDENCE ABOUNDS of the heavy drinking in the
United States during the late eighteenth and early
nineteenth centuries. For example, at a civic dinner for
eighty-five people at Plattsburgh, New York, in honor
of the victorious Lieutenant Thomas Macdonough,
who had just (1814) captured the British fleet on Lake
Champlain, seventeen regular toasts were drunk; beverages included two gallons of brandy, twenty of wine,
plus quantities of cider and porter. At Saratoga
visitors mixed alcohol with the mineral waters, which
may account for one of the early temperance societies
being established there. Hard liquor was included
among the rations at all army posts. Statistics of liquor consumption in the cities and on the Erie Canal
as well as shipments on roads, canals, and Lake Champlain add up to prodigious amounts of alcohol being
consumed by the relatively small population of the
day.

In those days Americans had a great fondness for solving any problem—you name it—by passing a law. As a matter of fact, they still do. Anyway, many years ago *some* Americans thought that *other* Americans were drinking too much and decided to do something about it. At first, though, they thought that voluntary efforts could solve the problem, and so temperance societies sprang up and pledges, such as the one above, were prepared.

The small band of nondrinkers soon decided, however, that people's lives were not being "improved" fast enough or in sufficient numbers to build a crime-and-poverty-free society. Their ranks were greatly augmented by the religious revivals of the 1820s and 1830s. It was not so much that the great revivalists, like Charles Grandison Finney, attacked alcohol as that they inspired others to battle all the social ills of the day. Multifaceted reform movements were the result. The temperance people stepped up their goal from merely less drinking to no drinking at all. This is typified by a small New York temperance society which is reputed to have put a large "T" beside the names of its members who pledged not to touch alcohol, thus originating the term "teetotaller."

The reformers gathered recruits rapidly, spearheaded by Protestant clergy and Neal Dow of Maine, with sensationalism added by the Washingtonians, a society of reformed drunkards who regaled their audiences with the horrors of *delirium tremens,* and by Timothy S. Arthur's *Ten Nights in a Bar-Room.* Because the socially active women of the day were fighting for the goals of higher education, admission to the professions, and legal and property rights, the reformers were mostly men. After Neal Dow's success of 1851 in obtaining prohibition in Maine, twelve other states went "dry" during the next six years, and New York nearly followed suit. A bill for statewide prohibition, passed by a Whig legislature in 1853, was vetoed by Democratic Governor Horatio Seymour as unconstitutional. A similar attempt two years later was voided by the courts on the same grounds. New York then resorted to local option to control the liquor traffic.

The turmoil of the era of Civil War and Reconstruction, however, not only put an end to further attempts at Prohibition but even resulted in the repeal of most of the states' prohibition laws. Not until the last quarter of the century were the circumstances right to fan the sparks of prohibition into flames again. Prohibitionists seemed to spring out of the shrubbery; the Women's Christian Temperance Union (WCTU) was founded in 1874, several Protestant temperance societies sprang up, and in 1898 the Anti-Saloon League was organized.

By the 1890s New Yorkers were supporting a Prohibition party. Although it did not win significant elections, it took away enough votes from the Republicans to enable the Democrats to elect their candidates. David Hill probably won the governorship by this means. He took a strong stand for "personal liberty," by which he meant the right of an individual to drink without interference from government. A majority of New Yorkers evidently agreed with him at that time.

Despite New York's reluctance, the prohibition movement was not to be stopped. By 1900 three states had total prohibition; the others operated under some form of local option. The WCTU and the Anti-

Saloon League were national in scope, determined, well organized, and abundantly financed. Women, although they did not yet have the right to vote, had learned how to make their voices heard. They produced several sensational spokeswomen such as Carrie Nation in Kansas, who struck a blow against Demon Rum by smashing up saloons with an axe. Members of the WCTU fought alcohol in the name of Christianity, and they had the ready cooperation of most of the Protestant clergy. Organized as early as 1874 in Plattsburgh, the group had its own column in the local paper, brought in noted speakers, publicly attacked the sellers of alcoholic beverages, and conducted an intensive educational campaign through the Sunday schools. The local secretary, Frances Hall, was instrumental in organizing several other units around the county. There must have been hundreds of such women across the country. The Anti-Saloon League exerted enormous pressure on politicians at all levels. If they were antiprohibitionist they were made to seem at best misguided, and at worst supporters of the Devil.

Early in the twentieth century two events intervened which gave the prohibition movement unexpected assistance. The first was the burgeoning of the Progressive Movement which flailed lustily away at all social ills, one of which was thought to be the consumption of alcohol. Eight states came to view liquor as an evil and were dry by 1909, nineteen by 1916. By the time national Prohibition went into effect, thirty-two states had been dried up. This left sixteen still operating under local-option laws, of which New York was one.

The other event which helped prohibition on its

way was World War I, and now for the first time the federal government swung into action. Its first step, in 1917, was to try to keep soldiers and alcohol apart. Next, it tried to conserve grains for the war effort by regulating the amounts that could be used in alcoholic beverages and by reducing the alcoholic content of beer to 2.75 percent from the prewar average of 3–3.5 percent. Then it legislated national prohibition for the duration of the war and demobilization. These acts can be considered a part of the war effort on at least three levels: the conservation of grains, the denial of grain to beer brewers, many of whom suffered because of their German names, and the sobering of the nation to meet the exhausting demands of a great war.

Since all these measures were temporary, Congress sent a Prohibition amendment to the states. Ratified by the necessary thirty-six states on January 16, 1919, it was to go into effect one year from that date. To be ready for the big day, Congress adopted the Volstead Act over President Woodrow Wilson's veto. It banned *all* intoxicating beverages and stringently defined the intoxicating level as an alcoholic content of more than one half of one percent. A few months later, Vice President Marshall told the Virginia Bar Association that Prohibition would not have received twenty votes if the Senate had voted behind closed doors. In 1922 Congressman L. D. Volk declared that the Volstead Act would be immediately repealed if congressmen voted as they drank. Be that as it may, John Barleycorn died a legal death at midnight on January 16, 1920, and the country embarked upon "an experiment noble in motive," as President Herbert Hoover later called it.

In retrospect, the optimism with which the government faced the problems of enforcement seems incredibly naive. At first the United States–Canadian border was solely in the hands of the customs and immigration officers who had enforced the pre-Prohibition laws. Only gradually were their numbers augmented to cope with the flagrant violations that began almost immediately. Roy Delano, former customs inspector of Rouses Point, New York, recalls that customs officers were so inadequately equipped at the start that they often hired taxis for their night patrols. Yet in August 1920, Federal Prohibition Commissioner John F. Kramer predicted that New York State would be dry in another month. In January 1921, he announced that the drinking of liquor had begun to taper off, and he was confident that the appetite would disappear entirely. But Major George F. Chandler, superintendent of the New York State Police, outdid even Kramer. In April he mandated a dry state in sixty days, and his schedule called for the drying up of fifty towns a week! This optimism was shown to be inflated when the statistics of enforcement in 1920 were reported. During this first year of Prohibition $10 million in liquor, 800 autos, and 3,000 stills were seized in New England and New York alone, and 10,000 persons arrested.

Settling down for a longer battle, state and federal governments slowly mobilized the agencies for enforcement. In 1921 New York invigorated its new Prohibition law with a large increase in the number of State Police and the establishment of a station for Troop B in Malone. The federal officers at the border gradually were provided with high-powered cars, usually the best of the vehicles seized from rumrunners.

In 1924 a Customs Marine Patrol was established to watch the water fronts, such as Lake Champlain, until a Coast Guard fleet could be acquired for the purpose. In the mid-1920s a specially trained federal police force was created—the United States Immigration Border Patrol, known as the Border Patrol. Its particular assignment was the arrest of aliens illegally entering the country, but under Prohibition the officers also guarded against all violations of federal laws at the border, including the bootlegging of liquor.

Investments in enforcement were made reluctantly by economy-minded Republican Congresses and administrations. Although Congress supplemented the Volstead Act with increasingly stringent measures, its annual debates over appropriations rarely produced the amount of money enforcement officials thought was minimal for adequate border protection. For example, when Prohibition was one month old the House of Representatives unanimously turned down an appropriation of $1 million to hire 1,000 guards for the Mexican and Canadian borders. Yet appropriations did inch up each year. From a sum of $7.1 million for fiscal 1921, the figure rose to $13.3 million for 1927, and it was increased somewhat in succeeding years. Despite its penny-pinching, Congress remained overwhelmingly dry until the end of the Prohibition years, and easily warded off all attempts to weaken the Volstead Act.

President Warren G. Harding, whatever his private beliefs and practices, was publicly committed to uphold the law as best he could. President Calvin Coolidge was, for him, loquacious on the subject. Although he never said he liked Prohibition, he rang changes on the theme that "there is no such thing as liberty without observance of the law"; "It is the duty of the citizen to observe the law and the duty of the Executive to enforce. I propose to do my duty as best I can." At Paul Smith's, New York, a village near Saranac Lake with a famous hotel where he vacationed in 1926, Coolidge allowed himself a glimpse of the future. He had concluded, he said, that Prohibition was here to stay, whatever its merits; modification of the law was out of the question, and consequently strict enforcement was the only issue.

But enforcement baffled the courts with the legal problems it created, although some of them were trivial—do trousers constitute a vehicle when they contain a hip flask? Others were more serious. Doctors' prescriptions for medicinal liquors were difficult to regulate, even after prescriptions for medical beer were outlawed in 1921. Warrants for raids and arrests remained troublesome issues for years. The alleged bribery of enforcement officers and their use of firearms sent civilian blood pressure soaring, while cries of anguish over double jeopardy followed state and federal prosecutions for the same offense.

The Supreme Court dealt with some of these issues in ways that gave comfort to the drys. At the beginning of Prohibition, states challenged the federal power to define intoxicating beverages as an invasion of their own police power. The Court in 1920 unanimously upheld the Volstead Act, including the authority to define the intoxicating content of liquor; concurrent powers did not yield the state any similar authority. In 1924 the Court upheld the constitutionality of the Willis-Campbell Act, which outlawed pre-

8

scriptions for beer for medicinal purposes. Two years later it refused to acknowledge double jeopardy in state and federal prosecutions for the same offense, because there could be violations of two different laws.

Prohibition in New York State had a hide-and-seek quality that makes it a fascinating study in itself. Alfred E. Smith, who was governor in 1919–20 and again from 1923–28, was a monumental force for states' rights and freedom of individual conscience. Having failed in 1919 and 1920 to persuade the legislature to ratify the Prohibition amendment only after a state-wide referendum, he encouraged a test of the state's authority under the Volstead Act. After a sensational battle, the same legislature that had ratified the Eighteenth Amendment in 1919 passed the Walker-Gillett bill in 1920 to legalize 2.75 percent beer. New York City Republicans lined up with Democrats to push it through. After passage, the halls of the Capitol reverberated to "How Dry I Am." Happy days were brief, however, because only two weeks later the Supreme Court, in effect, invalidated the law.

Nathan L. Miller, the Republican governor from 1921–22, promised during his campaign to enforce Prohibition fully. His first move was to get rid of the Walker-Gillett Act. He then sponsored a series of bills collectively known as the Mullan-Gage Act, which easily passed both houses of the legislature. The Act wrote the Volstead Act into state law but added even more far-reaching provisions. State officers might search for and seize liquor wherever it was suspected. Maximum penalties under the law were $1,000 or one year for a first offense and $2,000 or five years for the second. A person could sue for damages if injured in person, property, or means of support as the result of actions by an intoxicated individual. This drastic act committed every city policeman, sheriff's department, and troop of State Police to root out rumrunning in all forms. Governor Miller called for vigorous enforcement of this law and substantially increased the numbers of State Police.

But the Mullan-Gage Act was only one chapter in the saga of Prohibition in New York. Al Smith defeated Miller for re-election in the fall of 1922, and opposed as ever to Prohibition, Smith made no effort to conceal his opinions. Diane Filion of Champlain reports that he occasionally bought liquor at her door when he was passing through. On his return to the governor's office he had hardly recovered his breath from denouncing the Volstead Act when a measure to repeal Mullan-Gage reached the legislature. Known as the Dunnigan bill, it passed the Senate by a vote of 28–21 after a heated debate, but in the Assembly it failed by one vote when one expected Republican did not appear. Assemblyman James P. Nugent was getting a shave in a nearby barbershop, and he arrived at the Capitol just as the vote was completed. A motion to reconsider having been lost, the Cuvillier bill was immediately introduced to accomplish the same purpose. It passed the Assembly by a vote of 76–71 and the Senate by 28–22. Needless to say, the governor signed it. Henceforth, enforcement activities in New York State would rest primarily with federal officers.

During the debate roads leading from the border rang with the happy cry of the bootlegger (originally a person who hid a liquor bottle in the leg of his boot), who revved up his motor to deliver liquor in New York

City before the expected collapse in prices. Canadian distillers smugly confirmed that large export orders for beer and whiskey had been booked in a short time. Yet the wet era had not yet arrived, for the border was still manned by the same federal forces as before, together with the State Police.

Prohibition played havoc with American foreign relations. Numerous but minor problems arose over both liquor on foreign vessels while they were in American ports and transportation within the country of liquor for the use of foreign embassies. Canada posed the greatest quandary because of its three-thousand-mile border with the United States. One Canadian commentator at the start of Prohibition asserted that serious enforcement would require an armed guard every hundred yards from Vancouver to Winnipeg, and fifty feet everywhere else. Despite this exaggeration, Canadian authorities counted fifty roads in the Lake Champlain district alone, most of them without customs stations.

In 1920 eight Canadian provinces, including the Maritimes and Ontario, had their own prohibition laws. But the Ontario law was not enforced, and liquor was smuggled into the United States all along the St. Lawrence River and the Great Lakes. Discouraged by the problems this created, Ontario and five other provinces repealed their statutes during the 1920s.

The Quebec plan was generally used as a model for liquor control by the other provinces. Originating in Sweden and called the Gothenburg System, the plan created a Quebec Liquor Commission and government stores at which a customer was limited to the purchase of one bottle of liquor a day. Unlimited quantities of beer and wine could be purchased at private retail outlets. The Quebec system eventually gained the admiration of influential Americans who chafed under the restrictions of the Volstead Act. Nevertheless, the system came under attack. One provincial legislator accused the Liquor Commission of permitting, even encouraging, smuggling. Otherwise, he questioned, why should a second liquor store be established in Valleyfield, so near the border? Other people were disturbed by the lines of Americans at the government stores and the apparent unconcern of store managers over the many stratagems that were used to evade the one-bottle limit.

Until their own repeals, Quebec's dry neighbors were resentful of its prosperity. Tourists neglected the Maritimes or Ontario and flocked to Quebec in great numbers. Many new rooming houses were constructed in Quebec City and Montreal. Smugglers boosted the economy by their flagrant evasion of the one-bottle limit at government stores, while brewers and distillers strained their energies to keep up with the American demand.

By 1924 three new highways from Quebec into northern Vermont and New York were under construction, and Canadian officials admitted that money from thirsty American tourists and bootleggers was financing them and the new expenditures on education. Mounting sales of liquor at the province's eighty-six stores and mushrooming sales of wine and beer everywhere produced a windfall for the government. During the first three years of American Prohibition, the Quebec Liquor Commission took in $54.7 million. Of this, $19.1 million went to the federal government as taxes of $1.66 per bottle on whiskey the commission acquired for $1.33. The Quebec government pocketed $12.4 million in profits, and the figure climbed during the rest of the decade.

The United States was by far Canada's largest customer for alcoholic goods, more than 80 percent of Canada's exports going south of the border. By 1924 liquor exports were already valued at $14.8 million, and four years later their value exceeded $24 million. These were *legally cleared* shipments to the United States, not including wine and beer, and no one could guess the size of the undeclared shipments, which included most of the bootlegged liquor. One Canadian official declared that "the only limit to the amazing amount of liquor which may be legally shipped from Canada to the United States is the capacity of Canadian breweries and distilleries."

Under these circumstances, the American secretary of state repeatedly sought the cooperation of the Canadian government in stemming the flow, rather naively expecting Canada to forfeit a profitable enterprise. Numerous conferences produced two major treaties and several lesser agreements between the two nations, but Canadian officials reacted with less than complete enthusiam to some of the American requests, pointing out that enforcement was the primary responsibility of the United States and that failure was inevitable while the penalities for violation remained so low. Canadians said openly that if the American states wanted to stop the flow of liquor they could do so very easily. In 1929 Minister of National Revenue W. D. Euler questioned why Canada should help another nation enforce its laws—"United States authorities are making no very earnest effort to do it themselves."

Despite these reservations plus the full knowledge of the dollar profits involved, Canadian authorities did from time to time make gestures of limited cooperation. In part they were responding to repeated and urgent requests from a big neighbor, but they were also waking up to the disagreeable fact that smuggling *into* Canada was on the increase, with a consequent breakdown in Canadian law enforcement and the loss of considerable revenue. American bootleggers, who were already breaking the laws of one country, saw no reason to observe those of Canada. Where once they went back to Canada with empty cars and boats, they now found double profit from smuggling in both directions. Silks stolen in New York City had a ready sale on the Canadian black market. Canada was not collecting the 42.5 percent duty on the product, and furthermore its own silk industry was being undermined. Cigarettes also flowed northward illegally, as did alcohol. Industrial alcohol, recooked in the United States and smuggled into Canada, could be sold to distilleries for much less than Canadian alcohol, and it evaded all Canadian excises and threatened the legitimate industry.

With a serious problem of its own, the Canadian government was somewhat more receptive to pleas for help from Washington. In November 1923 an American mission to Ottawa brought requests for many things, including an extradition agreement and a Canadian promise to refuse legal clearance for its boats headed for the United States with liquor. The Canadians rejected an extradition treaty, although they did sign a treaty in 1924 which was much less than Americans had hoped for. It called for an exchange of information on the clearance of vessels (but not the refusal of clearances), the names and activities of suspected smugglers, and mutual help with witnesses and other trial procedures.

And still the two-way smuggling continued. In 1925 a Canadian delegation went to Washington for discussions, where Secretary of State Kellogg renewed earlier requests on extradition and ship clearances. He obtained neither, but the treaty of 1924 was strengthened by a promise of tighter Canadian rail and customs regulations. A better system was devised for notifying American authorities that shipments were on the way; coordination between agents of the two countries was supposed to help identify the spots where most of the illegal liquor flowed.

The Liberal government of Prime Minister Mackenzie King fell in 1926 over its alleged failure to check smuggling into Canada, with its consequent threat to the economy (one opposition leader charged that the Dominion had lost $200 million because of smuggling). King soon returned to power but not because the problem had been solved. In January 1929, another conference was held in Ottawa. Kellogg still hoped for extradition and a refusal of clearances for liquor-carrying vessels, but these would have required special Canadian legislation, for which no sentiment was apparent, especially in Quebec. A sharp difference of opinion developed between King and a member of his own government, W. D. Euler. King recommended the outlawing of liquor exports to the United States. Euler opposed the measure because the refusal of clearances would drive even legitimate business underground. Canada was already spending $1 million a year, he pointed out, to prevent smuggling from the United States, which did not deny clearances to its own vessels. Since almost all the smuggling was done by American citizens, he believed that the United States should institute controls over shipping along its own shores.

This Canadian-American preoccupation with smuggling by boat neglected the equally serious problem of smuggling by roads and railroads. In any case, there was little likelihood of controlling the hundreds of small craft that plied the waters of the Great Lakes, the St. Lawrence, and Lake Champlain. An attempt was made, nevertheless, by a treaty concluded in 1930, in which the United States promised to block the shipping of contraband into Canada while Canada undertook to halt the liquor traffic into the United States, each expecting to achieve its goal by refusing clearances. King declared that it would "enable us to control our officials in such a manner as to prevent them from cooperating individually and directly with bootlegging and rumrunners." Sharply challenged by the opposition, he admitted that "the rumrunners are mostly Americans, but if we are going to cooperate with any element in the United States, let us cooperate with the respectable element."

Since most of the smuggling into and out of Canada has always been underground, much of it on land, and since no large increases in enforcement personnel were provided by either country, the treaty failed to halt the smugglers' activities. A major loophole was discovered in the Canadian procedures, which were designed to deny clearances to countries with prohibition restrictions. A shipper in Canada merely obtained an export certificate for St. Pierre and Miquelon or some other legitimate destination, cleared Canadian waters, and then landed at an American port unchallenged. For as long as American Prohibition lasted neither Canada nor the United States solved the smuggling problems along their border. Indeed, even after the repeal of Prohibition smuggling continued to cast a long shadow over international relations when the United States tried to collect from Canada for the millions in lost revenue on liquor which had been allowed to leave Canada.

Heyday of the Bootlegger

*From the border as far down as Glens Falls we knew
all the back roads. After that we didn't.*

Gaston Monette of Rouses Point

*One time we went to 95th Street in New York
and when we drove up in front there were two policemen there. They helped us carry the beer and whiskey into this cabaret.*

Sam Racicot of Rouses Point

*I've had some that [were] so close they're al-
most scatching my back. The law shot the tires out
from under the car and I had to jump it, and I had to
jump it right close to where their car was.*

Gaston Monette

TWENTY-YEAR-OLD BILLY hummed a lively tune as he
drove his old Dodge car south toward Chazy. If he did
say so himself, he had just put on a good performance
at the Canadian border. The result might have been
quite different, he knew, because he was carrying ten
burlap bags of beer. At the border he was stopped and
questioned, as he had known he would be. Of course it
helped to be recognized as the son of a prominent citizen of Plattsburgh, but he thought it also helped to
project a friendly, candid personality which he had
developed over the months of his new career—
bootlegging.

19

He knew that although the border was the most crucial part of his journey, he still faced hazards on his way south. For example, Miner's Woods were just ahead. Was there a trap awaiting him there? And what about the city of Plattsburgh or Poke-O'-Moonshine? If he got through safely this time, perhaps he should vary his routine on the next trip and not appear at the same place too often. So far he had been lucky.

Men like Billy went into rumrunning for many reasons, including money and prestige. In the early years some young men had just been released from the army, with no jobs in sight. A few ex-troopers and patrolmen turned to bootlegging in protest against what they conceived as unfair treatment or against society in general. But for many of the younger bootleggers the thrill of the work was more satisfying than the money. The excitement of a successful chase was enough to make them go back to Canada again and again. Bucky Ladd, whose father was the respected head of customs at Rouses Point, had a profitable brokerage business there which he neglected in favor of the more risky profits of bootlegging. Francis "Sam" Racicot, a bootlegger in Rouses Point as a young man, puts into words what he and his friends did not then: "Most of the bootleggers considered that it was an unfair law and a law which had been foisted on us, which had no validity. We knew that it wasn't being supported by the general public, that it was disliked, and that we didn't feel we were lawbreakers."

Numerically, the largest group was the petty smugglers, who had vacationed in Canada or had visited the border night spots and wanted to return home with a bottle or two. If caught at the border, they were usually relieved to get off with a small fine and the loss of the liquor. Occasionally, a man like Thomas McBeetry of Saranac Lake refused to pay the five dollar fine even when his companions did so, and too late found himself held in $1,000 bail for a session of federal court. An unexpected by-product of this traffic was the shipping of carloads of American-made pint flasks to Canada for sale to American tourists. The United Cigar Stores in Quebec became almost too busy to sell any tobacco.

In the towns along the border, teenagers comprised another category of smugglers. Elmer Caron, later sheriff of Clinton County, recalls how the boys of Churubusco used to buy a little beer at Toissant Trombly's across the border: "An officer once stopped a group of them on their return and found one bottle. The boys were considered innocent of smuggling but they were thoroughly frightened." Howard Curtis remembers that as a schoolboy in Mooers a sixteen-year-old classmate once asked him to cut school and go to the movies in Plattsburgh in his Model T. When they reached town they drove into a garage, where some cases were unloaded from the rear seat, and then they went to the show. Howard discovered that at about the age of fifteen he had unwittingly been a party to beer-running, "my only participation that I know of at this time."

The seventeen-year-old son of a member of the Board of Education in Utica came north in search of adventure and money. Another boy of the same age arrived on foot at the Sanger home on Rand Hill, recalls Ralph Sanger. Cold and wet, he had been forced to abandon his load and run into the snow-covered woods. Ralph's mother gave him breakfast while she lectured him on the foolishness of his ways, as she did others who came to her door.

Herbert St. John of Plattsburgh, age seventeen, was held under heavy bail for federal court after attempting to run beer. He sideswiped a car in the city, lost control, and went into the ditch where his car overturned, hurling him through the top. In addition to reckless driving, he was also charged with operating without license or plates. A resident of Rouses Point remembers that he started smuggling beer at the age of sixteen. He and a friend bought a case apiece in Canada and carried it on their backs through the pastures and woods. They obtained it cheaply and doubled their money in Rouses Point. By making two or three trips a night, they could make a profit of several dollars. Their next step was to buy a horse. Baskets on each side of the animal held two cases apiece. The boys each carried a case and led the horse, and two trips a night gave them good returns. Two other Rouses Point youths, ages fifteen and twenty, were not so lucky, for they were caught while carrying ale on their backs.

It was men in their twenties and thirties, however, who accounted for most of the volume of smuggled goods. One group was the self-employed who owned their own cars. Most towns had several of them, and they were often good friends who shared their fun and information with each other. Yet on the road they were usually lone wolves, traveling by themselves and seeking their own markets.

Another group included the eager beavers who could be hired to drive a load across the border. When they did so they became a part of an enterprise organized by professionals from Saratoga, Glens Falls, or New York City. The car might be furnished for them, but more often they used their own. They were paid either fifty dollars a week and expenses, ten dollars a day, a flat rate per trip, or a case of liquor. At a time when a day's pay in other work was only $1.50-2.00, bootlegging seemed a quick way to get rich. The money enabled them to dress snappily, their wardrobes invariably including a coonskin coat, and gave them some distinction among their peers.

Sometimes the contacts between professional and driver were accidental. A Plattsburgh youth once went to a dance in Rouses Point where he was propositioned to bring a load of liquor from Canada. He attempted it, got through, and subsequently made regular trips for his employer. But there were also places like the Union Hotel in Plattsburgh, which were known as meeting places of professionals and drivers, as recalled by Darwin Keysor of Plattsburgh, who clerked there during high-school. There the drivers got their instructions, and after a successful trip they were treated to a steak dinner and given a great deal of flattering attention, "and they thought they were big shots." The professional could afford to do this because he could anticipate good profits downstate while at the same time running almost no risk himself. But the driver, if caught, could expect no help, and he would almost certainly lose his car, liquor, and perhaps his freedom.

Regional hierarchies were important in the bootlegging fraternity. The "king" of bootleggers won the title by unusually daring and successful exploits. Dick

Warner of Saratoga seems to have been the first, but his eventual arrest and jailing left the field open to other hopefuls. The "queen" of bootleggers was a female counterpart. For a while Dorothy Swartout of Saratoga was the unchallenged title-holder. She and Warner shared many adventures on the northern border. While the less daring might hope to be known as "baron" or "duke," none of these terms meant much in northern New York.

The main roads of Clinton County fanned out from Lacolle and Hemmingford to Rouses Point, Champlain, and Mooers and then converged as they approached Plattsburgh. Smugglers coming into Champlain could join the "Rum Trail" (Route 9) at Chazy or go by way of Perrys Mills and Mooers to Route 22, which took them south through West Chazy and Beekmantown to Plattsburgh. Many rumrunners, however, avoided the city by a variety of other routes. Those starting south on Route 22 could leave it at Mooers or West Chazy and get onto the Military Turnpike. This road bypassed Plattsburgh and rejoined Route 22 north of Peru, and it ran past an important storage depot at the Sunrise Hotel, on the corner of the Turnpike and Route 3. The other trail started at Hoyt's loading station on the border north of Mooers Forks and ran south through Woods Falls, Altona, Rand Hill, and Morrisonville to Peru. This route also had a storage depot, the Hotel Chanticler at the intersection of routes 3 and 22B.

At Keeseville many bootleggers, in order to avoid traps in the mountains at Poke-O'-Moonshine, went to Au Sable Forks and rejoined Route 9 south of Elizabethtown. From there the "Rum Trail" led to

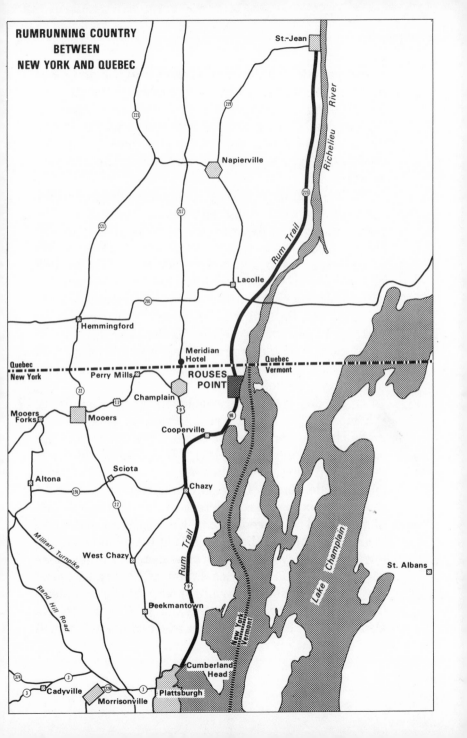

Saratoga, Glens Falls, and Albany, and the danger of interception was less but not completely absent. One enterprising Plattsburgh taxi driver who also ran regular loads to Saratoga bought a cornfield on the north edge of town. By cutting two rows of corn, he could glide into Saratoga without using the main approach.

If nothing else, the techniques developed by bootleggers were imaginative and ingenious. The petty smugglers often risked concealment of liquor on their persons. Pockets were used, but so were less obvious places. Men had belts made especially to hold bottles, and false vests with pockets large enough for a pint bottle each. Women, who were often expected to run the risks for their male partners, concealed liquor in their bloomers as well as under their corsets. A large person could more successfully disguise odd bulges than a small one, and the loose clothing styles of the day also helped.

Border residents developed some smuggling schemes in the best rural tradition. A Mooers cow made the rounds with her owner between Hemmingford, Mooers, and Champlain. "This dutiful old cow," as Howard Curtis describes her, carried a bale of hay on each side. Finally Officer John O'Hara, who seemed to have a sixth sense in detection, became suspicious of an animal that needed to be bred so often, and upon examining the hay discovered that each bale was hollow and filled with bottles of whiskey. Horses were also put to good use. Leo Filion of Champlain, who was in the business of rumrunning himself, remembers one owner who lost three horses by gunfire. He also tells of a Champlain farmer who had horses trained as bootleggers. He could load one with liquor in Canada and turn it loose, confident that it would avoid all human contact and find its way home through the woods. A great deal of local smuggling was done on foot or snowshoes or with toboggans. Filion remembers a man who could carry four cases at a time on his back. "That would be four dozen bottles and would have weighed more than one hundred pounds," he points out.

But these homely methods hardly sufficed to smuggle goods in the quantity the market demanded, so concealment in cars was tried and found amazingly successful. Sometimes nothing mechanical had to be done to the vehicle. The Mooers undertaker found his hearse perfectly suited to a sideline in smuggling. He always had all the necessary papers for crossing the border, presumably with a body in the coffin. But Officer O'Hara began to wonder about the sudden rise in the death rate, and when he opened the casket he found no body, but plenty of liquor.

Most car owners did not have the natural advantages of the hearse. Some thought that driving without lights or plates shielded them from discovery at night, even though they created hazards for other travelers when they persisted in driving fifty miles an hour. Rumrunners learned to use cars with reinforced springs to support heavy loads. They found that they could wire liquor under the car, or conceal it behind or under seats, in tool boxes, and in spare tires or trunks. They rebuilt cars with false floors of tin through which lengthened pedals and shifting levers were devised; this created a space large enough to store twenty quarts of liquor. Another ruse was the false gas tank.

This Hudson coach seized by Inspector John P. Ross at Rouses Point, N.Y., is equipped with a compartmentalized gas tank. The center filler hole was used to smuggle almost twelve gallons of liquor in a special copper tank. The lower hole took a small amount of gasoline, necessitating frequent refills.

The tank was divided so that one part carried a little gas, but the other part could hold many quarts of liquor. Still another was a false top. Cars of the day were made with fabric tops, and between two layers of fabric a storage space four inches deep was constructed that could carry 180 pints of liquor. Such a

Another view of the copper tank with the cap screwed on.
The trunk and trunk deck placed over it helped to conceal it.

top seems to have been the specialty of a garage in
Napierville, Quebec.

On the other hand, some bootleggers became
convinced that they were less likely to be stopped if
they rode openly about their business with tops down.
Any speeding car with its top up and side curtains on
certainly was bound to invite suspicion. Yet no
method was foolproof. A car once pulled up at customs
at Rouses Point bearing two adults and six children.
Not a bottle was in sight, yet a search revealed that

Shown propped against the rear wheel of the car, this smugglers' tank took the place of the rear seat springs and was then covered with the upholstery to disguise it.

two tunnels had been built running the length of the drive shaft, in which 480 quarts of Canadian ale were concealed.

Bootleggers who wanted to be prepared in case of pursuit provided themselves with a means of making smoke. Some pumped oil into the exhaust. Others used a fire extinguisher filled with a chemical; the pump was bolted to the door of the car and the nozzle connected with a tube running to the exhaust chamber. One or two charges were enough to lay a dangerous smoke screen. Still others had an air-compression machine which stirred up the dust of the road. A smoke screen was illegal, dust was not, yet it was often as effective.

In the winter, whether the roads were open or not, much smuggling was done by sleigh. This traffic was quite safe because it was conducted across the fields away from the patrolled highways. Almost all farmers had flat-bottomed sleighs which they used to haul potatoes and other produce to market. But in winter they were inclined either to do a little bootlegging themselves or rent their conveyances to others. Some bootleggers also took their loads across the ice of Lake Champlain. They did not always remember to check the thickness of the ice, and in February 1924, two men and a sleighload of Canadian ale went into seven feet of water in Trombly's Bay. With help from ashore, horses and sleigh were saved, but the neighbors had to wait until spring to bring up the beer with hooks.

Sleighs were good only for slow, local traffic. Bootleggers kept their cars on the road except after heavy snows and high winds, and even then they tried to keep some of the back roads open for their own use. Diane Filion recalls doing some of this work for her friends with her new Ford; then, she says, customs officers planted two bottles of whiskey on the car and seized it: "I decided not to make a legal case of it because even if I won, my life would be intolerable afterwards."

Informal intelligence networks were organized by the bootleggers. One variety employed youngsters to watch the customs house, especially at night. When the officers left on patrol, the boys either signalled or telephoned to a loading spot across the border that the coast was clear. Youngsters were also employed to follow a patrolman by motorcycle and telephone back the direction he took. In Rouses Point the telephone operator helpfully relayed information concerning the whereabouts of enforcement officers to bootleggers who called in.

Once across the border the bootlegger had a choice of roads. He also had a choice of procedures. He might decide to make a run for it on his own. If he was part of an organization he joined a caravan, which sent scouts ahead in a pilot car to make sure the road was clear. If the pilot car was stopped no harm was done because it was "clean." If it was not challenged for ten to twenty miles, the driver telephoned back that the road was clear. The run, at least as far as Elizabethtown, was often plotted in advance, with farmers' barns or garages rented for quick concealment during a pursuit or as a rest stop while the pilot car scouted the next stretch of road. Farmers even flagged down bootleggers to warn them of danger ahead and to offer sanctuary. Normally, however, the barns were rented by the month. Patrolman Philip Auer reports that bootleggers once tried unwittingly to rent a garage from his wife.

An alternative to shipping liquor straight through to its destination was the use of storage depots in the Plattsburgh area. Sometimes the depots were farmers' barns and country hotels, just as often they were buildings within the city, constructed so that the bootleg car could drive inside to unload. Several garages on Peru Street, a barn on Prospect Avenue, and the Sunrise and Chanticler hotels west of town served this purpose. The liquor, sometimes in large quantities, was left in these places after a run from the border until arrangements could be made to move it south.

Smugglers were early drawn to the possibilities of the railroad. The small-timers, like those in automobiles, discovered many hiding places. They might tie an individual bottle to a string and hang it out of the window during customs inspection at Rouses Point. If the bottle broke the owner pulled in only a jagged bottle neck; sometimes it was only the string when local boys made off with the bottle, according to Sam Racicot. Liquor was also concealed in ventilators, light fixtures, the springs of Pullman seats, upper berths, and mattresses. Panels in staterooms and washrooms were unscrewed to provide hiding places. Trunks were constructed with false sides and bottoms where many pints could be stored. The so-called "suitcase brigade" consisted of those who simply tried to smuggle liquor in their personal luggage.

Large-scale smugglers, however, were intrigued with the possibilities of the freight car, which offered many advantages over smuggling by automobile. It could be made to carry a load fifty times that of a car. Trains were not stopped by winter weather. Furthermore, it was safer for both smuggler and receiver because false bills of lading made their identities impossible to discover even if the shipment was detected and seized. Bootleggers sometimes gained access to empty freight cars in Canada and constructed false ends three feet deep that created space for almost 200 cases of beer in each end. But just as often they shipped a full car of liquor billed as fish, lumber, hay, or lime. The car was loaded at Napierville or other railroad centers in Quebec and consigned to a receiver in New York or New Jersey. The liquor was concealed under a thin covering of the legitimate cargo named in the bill of lading, and a car could easily carry 100 to 150 barrels of beer. It was then sealed for the trip across the border. There was probably some connivance by Canadian railroad officials, but this was not necessary under the normal procedures for shipping by the carload.

The Merchants' Association of Montreal once traced a shipment of this kind and found that the shipper had negotiated with the railroad for the use of a car. He billed the shipment as baled hay, but three hundred bags of beer, each containing twenty-four bottles, were covered by the hay. The shipping cost was $1,700 plus $450–500 for routing, labor, and camouflage. The intended destination was Newburgh, New York, which would receive beer at a transportation cost of only thirty cents a quart.

Except in winter, Lake Champlain offered many opportunities for transporting liquor. With a rowboat or an outboard motorboat the small-time smuggler could shuttle back and forth all night. But the professionals used high-powered craft like Chrysler, Cris-Craft, and Grey, some of them elaborate twenty to forty-foot cruisers. Billy Hicks, one of the most active of the local bootleggers, owned a forty-foot boat which he painted black and used at night. When fully loaded it carried 300–400 cases of beer and was barely out of water. A favorite loading place was in the cove just north of Fort Montgomery, but boats could safely navigate the Richelieu River all the way from St. John.

There were man-made hazards on water as well as land. The swing bridge on the railroad across the lake always had to be opened for the larger craft and for almost all boats during high water in the spring. Some rumrunners went through nevertheless, but others unloaded near Rouses Point and continued their journey by land. There were also lake patrols. If a patrol boat approached, the smugglers dropped the liquor overboard so as not to be caught with the evidence.

A capacious device for smuggling by water was the "submarine," a low-lying craft without its own power. Towed behind a large boat, it was cut loose and allowed to sink during a pursuit. With luck the bootleggers could later return and recover the sunken craft; the floating rope would show them where it lay.

A similar device made use of a small wooden box of rock salt. If a pursuit became hot the bags of liquor were dropped overboard, each attached by a long rope to a box of salt. When the salt dissolved the box returned to the surface and guided smugglers to their lost goods.

There were also natural hazards on the lake. Engine failure was always a possibility. Customs officers easily seized a thirty-foot launch abandoned off Cumberland Head lighthouse when its engine stopped. Reefs and irregular shoreline were a danger to pilots unacquainted with the lake. Their threat was made worse by sudden, violent storms that sometimes ravaged the waters. Willsboro Point was such a place, and five bootleg boats came to grief there within a period

A seized rum boat at dock at Rouses Point, N.Y. The liquor, packed tightly in bags, was carried on the specially constructed shelves at the front of the craft so it could easily be pushed overboard during a pursuit.

of two years. The crew usually escaped, but their load and sometimes the boat went to the bottom of the lake.

A fifty-foot cabin cruiser once left Plattsburgh for Vermont with 3,000 bottles of ale aboard. Off Port Kent the operator stripped its gears and two of the crew went ashore to look for new parts, leaving a third man on board. A gale sprang up and the smuggler dropped anchor, but lost it. The boat was blown northward until it struck a reef near Providence Island. The man jumped overboard and swam ashore in November waters. Meanwhile, the other two had obtained a steam yacht in which they searched the lake for the missing cruiser. When they finally found it, the storm prevented them from rescuing much of the cargo, and when they returned the next day, agents were waiting to apprehend them. The cruiser was scattered along the shore for more than a mile, completely fragmented.

The large stocks of liquor on hand in the United States made smuggling in quantity unnecessary during the early months of Prohibition, recalls Roy Delano. Aged British and Canadian whiskey, often carried in charred oak barrels, was eventually smuggled in to blend with the raw American product and stimulate the aging process. But the growing thirst could not be quenched by illegally made American products, and by 1921 large-scale smuggling of foreign bottled goods was under way.

The market for alcoholic beverages was almost universal, but bootleggers preferred the centers of population. The speakeasies of Rouses Point and Plattsburgh tapped into the flow, although the large markets and high prices were to be found in Glens Falls, Saratoga, Albany, and New York. Profits from smuggling depended upon the kind of liquor, the place of sale, and the number of people who had to share the proceeds. The individual operator could buy beer in Canada for $4.50 or $5.00 a case and sell it in Plattsburgh for $10.00. By carrying it to New York, he could get up to $25.00. Two trips a week were feasible in summer, one in winter if the road was open. If he took a small carload of twenty-five cases, a smuggler could make as much as $600 a run, less his expenses. When smuggling was the work of an organization, the added costs included the relays of drivers, storage charges near the border (up to $3.00 a case), and the rental of barns and storage depots along the way. These expenses were trifling considering the large volume of alcohol that a professional could keep moving.

The most popular Canadian beer in the United States was probably Molson's, closely followed by Black Horse Ale, Carling's Red Label, and Labatt's. Favorites among the whiskies were 3-Star Hennessy, Canadian Club, and White Horse Scotch. Bootleggers in Rouses Point sometimes took telephone orders for specific champagnes or whiskies for special occasions in downstate cities.

Champagne could be bought in Canada for $4–7 a bottle and might bring up to $20 in New York. Rye was available for $4, brought $7–9 in Plattsburgh and $12 in New York, for a profit of $8. Scotch provided a $12 mark-up. When it was available, pure alcohol was also profitable. Canadian businessmen were allowed to buy and store it for industrial purposes at ninety-eight cents a gallon. Sam Racicot found a perfume manufacturer who was willing to sell it for $2. He and Roy Ashline would "go through this little false door and pull out the five-gallon tins and load them in the car and head directly for the border and take them down to New York." There they sold it for $15 a gallon. But by 1923 New York City was being so well supplied with hard liquor by the "Rum Row" of offshore boats that overland whiskey began to lose its biggest market.

A bootlegger from New Rochelle, N.Y., drove this Auburn 120 into Canada periodically and returned exuding respectability but carrying thirty cases of whiskey. It was packed in the trunk, behind and under the back seat, and in the tool drawers on the side of the car. *Courtesy of Bertha Monette.*

Whiskey bought in Canada cost only a little less than it did offshore, and it was still 325 miles away. So beer and ale came to preempt almost 75 percent of all smuggling across northern New York except during the coldest winter months, when whiskey became temporarily popular because it was less likely to freeze.

Bootleggers wanted a fast car and one capable of carrying 25–40 cases of liquor. Cadillacs, Packards,

The Auburn 120 with the top down. *Courtesy of Bertha Monette.*

Pierce Arrows, and Marmons were highly regarded, although every kind was used in the trade, and beginners had to be satisfied with smaller and older cars. Bootleggers could buy cars through the usual retail outlets that other people used. They could also bid at government auctions of seized cars, but the wary decided that these cars were too well known by the patrolmen and would easily be recognized if they were put back into the smuggling business.

The major source of bootleggers' cars was, therefore, a stolen-car center in Albany. Cars were cheap, no questions were asked, and since the state had not developed registration procedures, only money and a simple bill of sale containing a fictitious name changed hands. In 1922 Sam Racicot bought a 1917 Cadillac there for $200, used it for a year, and sold it, after he had wrecked it, for his purchase price. Its top speed was fifty miles an hour, and up to sixty going downhill. The speed of the early cars has been exaggerated, and even if they had been capable of eighty miles an hour, which they were not, the condition of the roads would have made such speeds impossible. The Cadillac owner found that the hill out of Elizabethtown toward Keene was so steep that he had to go up in reverse. Gasoline was cheap, but tires were expensive. A bootlegger learned to carry spares because he could not expect much more than two months of use from the tires of the day.

Until the mid-twenties, bootleggers' cars returned to Canada empty. Then some of them began to realize that there were products worth smuggling into Canada which were as profitable as the liquor traffic southward. So they began to carry contraband in both directions. Raw alcohol was a favorite product to send north because of the high prices paid for it there. It could be obtained in New York and other large cities for $4–7 a gallon, transported in five-gallon tins, and sold to Canadian distillers for seventeen dollars. The profits of moving alcohol into Canada were greater than those of bringing liquor into the United States and consequently attracted a large number of smugglers. Until 1925 neither Canadian nor United States officials seemed aware of the scope of the northbound traffic, and so cars going into Canada were not carefully inspected. "That fact," according to Lieutenant Gonflo of the State Police in Malone, "together with the greater profits made the alcohol trade about the most attractive thing in the smuggling line. Ever since our line has tightened we have captured many rum smugglers who told us they have deserted the booze trail and given their entire time to the alcohol trade." According to him, one-half of the cars seized by the troopers in the summer of 1925 contained alcohol and were headed for Canada.

The traffic was big enough to make use of the railroads. One freight car seized in 1925 on the American side of the border near Malone carried alcohol valued at $7,500 and worth $18,000 in Canada. That same night hired gunmen from Albany tried unsuccessfully to distract the State Police and get the car over the border, two miles away. Montreal authorities in 1931 discovered a freight car from Albany containing eighty drums labelled "white oil." Only twenty contained oil, the rest had alcohol. This traffic included industrial alcohol and alcohol made from corn, both of which were made into cheap liquor in Canada and smuggled back into the United States. In this way illegal profits were made in both countries.

Smuggled commodities constituted a threat to Canada's tax structure and economy. Smugglers established a large traffic in silk stolen in New York City and transported to Canada without regard for customs regulations. Merchants and manufacturers in Montreal provided a ready market, and they never asked too many questions about its origin. One merchant obtained his silk by a second robbery at the border, whereupon he billed the railroad for the same material.

Other products smuggled northward were narcotics, tobacco, and cigarettes. By 1931 Canadian officials were singling out smuggled alcohol and narcotics as their most serious problem. The smuggling continued until the end of American Prohibition.

Conrad LaBelle, the notorious Canadian smuggler, carried liquor to New York and alcohol back to Canada and is reputed to have kept a fleet of twenty cars and drivers on the road. One of the boldest and toughest of his day, LaBelle personally took part in bootlegging, but he was never caught at customs on either side of the border.

Bootleggers sometimes found "kicks" and profit in thefts. For example, numerous impounded cars were recaptured. A typical operation went like this: two bootleggers, after a hot pursuit by customs officers, abandoned their load of beer and escaped into the fields. Their fast truck was seized and driven to Bursey's Garage in Rouses Point, where captured autos were often temporarily stored. Two nights later it was stolen, the thieves getting into the garage by smashing a glass in the side door.

Another kind of theft was from citizens who had stocked their cellars before Prohibition and established legal ownership by registering it with local Prohibition authorities. Charles Miller of Plattsburgh was such a victim when his cellar was raided. The stolen liquor was soon found, but while three city policemen guarded it, it was stolen again. It was recovered a second time, but the upshot of this unsavory business was the suspension of the three policemen and the jailing of three youths.

Impounded liquor always seemed a tempting

target. Elmer Caron tells of a load of beer that was seized and stacked near the railroad station in Churubusco. As he tells it: "A Mr. Wilson leaned on the pile to guard it, but despite his vigilance young men managed to remove a bag at a time from the rear of the pile." A citizen of Rouses Point, in whose cellar officers had placed eighty-one cases of liquor for safekeeping, reported twenty-seven of them gone and his horse missing. A cash reward was offered, but no one came forward to claim it. The Austin-Ryan Company in Plattsburgh was also used for customs storage. Twice in 1924 it was robbed of beer, entry being gained by an iron bar applied to the sliding doors.

Gaston Monette tells of the time that Hamilton McCrea, a respected customs officer, was driving a captured carload of liquor from the border back to the customs house in Rouses Point. It was nearly dark, but a crowd gathered to see the fun. According to Monette, a former bootlegger, "they took about half of the load out *while she was running.*" This feat was accomplished by a man riding on the front bumper of a car which closely followed McCrea. He reached into McCrea's car and pulled out full bags of liquor, dropping them off where everyone could help himself, and *"the law didn't notice it."*

The thefts that set the North Country agog were from the customs house at Rouses Point. Three robberies were the work of the same gang—Roy Ashline, Bucky Ladd, and Sam Racicot, who survives to tell the story. Bucky's father was the trustworthy head of the local customs. Bucky swiped one of his keys and made a copy that fitted the front door of the customs house. Late one night the three quietly entered the building and climbed the stairs, but they had no key to the "strong room," where the liquor was stored. One of them hoisted Sam through the transom, and they got away with twenty-two cases of the choicest whiskies, which had been saved from destruction and earmarked for hospitals, but which the gang sold in Plattsburgh at prime prices.

The theft caused a great disturbance because it was assumed that customs officers must have had a hand in it. Nevertheless, a few weeks later the group made another raid and got away with thirty-five cases, which they again sold in Plattsburgh. The gang looked upon their work as a "rescue" operation, not robbery. The second escapade caused an uproar, a visit by security officers from Syracuse, and the installation of new locks and bolts. But Roy and Sam made a third attempt. Lacking a key to the front door, they got in through a window in the half of the building housing the Myers brokerage firm. They again went through the transom, a method apparently not suspected at the time, and got away with forty-five cases. This time the loot was taken to New Rochelle. The robberies were expertly executed and their perpetrators were unknown, although customs officers remained under a thick cloud of suspicion.

Several years later, after he had moved to Montreal, Sam was visited by the head of internal security of American customs. The agent told Sam that he was a suspect but that there would never be any proof, and he asked him to tell his story under a guarantee of immunity from prosecution. Sam good-naturedly agreed to talk, except that he would name no accomplices. His train fare was paid to Syracuse, and he was provided with a good room and evening entertainment while he was there. He spent three days before a board of inquiry, answering questions and drawing diagrams. His fare was paid back to Montreal, and the government was able to clear up this nagging mystery.

Guns were a part of the equipment of many of the bootleggers from downstate but rarely of those from the North Country. The wilder and more desperate of the smugglers did not hesitate to shoot to maim or kill their pursuers, and shooting frays became commonplace along the border. It is probably true that the earliest deadly shooting was done by the bootleggers, and that patrolmen began to meet violence with violence in order to enforce the law.

Rumrunners had a number of advantages that lessened the hazards of their profession. The number of officers was insufficient to form more than a token patrol along the border, and bootleggers came to know the personal weaknesses of some of the officers and to exploit them. They also knew that some of them were less dedicated than others and were apt to show indulgence to petty or youthful offenders.

The terrain fitted the needs of the rumrunners. Northern New York was mostly rural, with occasional small towns between the border and Plattsburgh, twenty miles away. Numerous roads crossed the border, but only a few of them had customs stations. The many wooded areas along the highways offered refuge to bootleggers who abandoned their cars in flight; the great majority of them made good their escape, to be back in business a few days later.

Customs stations were closed at night, and the

border was unguarded except for the patrols. Serious bootleggers consequently learned to make their big runs after ten or eleven o'clock, when the stations were dark. Ralph Sanger remembers seeing a caravan of as many as fourteen cars pass his home on Rand Hill. A reporter for the *Plattsburgh Republican* conducted a series of interviews along the border in 1923 and documented the extent of this traffic. He was told in Mooers that thirty cars an hour passed through the village during the night. A caravan of fourteen cars had recently passed unchallenged through Mooers, the pilot having first stopped to ask a villager whether the road was clear ahead. Residents of Champlain and Mooers said that if they got up to look every time a car roared by, they would get no sleep. At about the time of the interviews, 132 cars passed the Rouses Point customs house in one night without stopping to report. The office was then being kept open to help conscientious people obtain proper clearance in and out of Canada. Bootleggers obviously never stopped; anyway, many used roads which avoided customs completely.

During the summer months, bootleggers had another bonus at the customs stations. Students from St. Lawrence University in Canton, New York, received temporary appointments as customs officers. Young and inexperienced, they could sometimes be fooled by the tricks of the old-timers. Bootleggers assert that they were even able to walk out of a station with a suitcase full of seized liquor, unrecognized and unchallenged. The margin of safety for the bootlegger was usually the degree of assurance and naturalness he could put into his actions.

The countryside was dotted with farmers who, if unwilling to rent their barns for storage, as many of them did, sympathized with the bootleggers, gave them tips, and provided temporary shelter. Nevertheless, according to Darwin Keysor, an occasional farmer double-crossed a bootlegger by telling him that someone had stolen his load. A well-known garage in Rouses Point, located about a block from the customs house, served the bootleggers well as a transfer point. A loaded Canadian car arriving at the edge of town was made to backfire and then crawled to the garage for help. Once inside, the liquor was transferred to an American car which was casually driven away unchallenged, while the "clean" Canadian car dutifully reported to customs down the street.

The life of a bootlegger would have been much harder without the many kinds of assistance he received near the border. At the other end of the "Rum Trail" bootleggers also testify to the numerous occasions that New York City policemen actually helped them unload and carry their contraband into the premises of a purchaser.

Houses astride the border were a special boon to the American who wanted to buy a drink, or to the smuggler who wanted a good loading place. The possession of liquor on the Canadian side of the line was legal, and if the line ran through the living room, American officers were foiled in every raid because the occupants merely had to move briskly to the other side of the room to be in another country. Not until border officers in both countries cooperated in padlocking the buildings and prohibiting the construction of more like them was the problem partially solved.

48

Bootleggers found that beer and liquor were available for the asking in Canada. Both Quebec authorities and private individuals were happy to capitalize on the windfall of American Prohibition. Loading stations for beer lined the Canadian side of the border. They were usually farms or hotels, where business was so brisk that the beer was stacked higher than the cars that came to pick it up. Operators obtained the beer at breweries farther north, brought it to the border, loaded it into bootleggers' cars, and provided a primitive spy service. For this they made a good profit. One farmer supplemented his income by emptying a bottle from every case and returning the cap. When he received complaints his answer was, "Well, when I gave it to you it was good; it must have been the ride down—the cap must have come out." Bootleggers generally bought beer packed in burlap bags of twenty-four bottles. They usually packed their own whiskey in the same way or carried it by the case.

Some of the loading stations were well-known Canadian night spots like the Meridian Hotel just north of Champlain and the Brass Knuckle over the border from Rouses Point. At both, drinks on the premises were also sold to a large American clientele. The Meridian maintained telephone connections by which the bootleggers kept informed about their chances at the border.

The Canadian beer industry was served by two groups of affiliated breweries, each producing almost half of the total national output. Both groups had plants to serve the licensed dealers along the border. One of these was at Napierville, only twelve miles from Rouses Point. In an average summer week this plant received from 23–35 freight cars of beer, each containing 900 cases of 24 bottles. A correspondent for the *New York Times* estimated that in 1925 some 10 million gallons of beer were shipped into the United States from the province of Quebec alone. The provincial output increased by at least 10 percent annually.

Another Canadian headquarters for the New York trade was Valleyfield, Quebec, which became a center where stolen or smuggled cars were swapped for liquor for the American market. Two or three stolen cars crossed the line from New York every night. In Valleyfield whiskey was exchanged for a car at about one-fifth of its value, but the operation still produced a profit to the smuggler of $1,500–2,000 per trip. The new Canadian owner of the car changed its external appearance and sold it a couple of months later for $1,000–1,500.

Wines were as easily available as beer in Quebec, but liquor required a different procedure. Quebec operated its own liquor stores where the law allowed the purchase of only one bottle a day per customer. Border entrepreneurs stockpiled whiskey and other liquors for bootleggers by hiring many people to make multiple purchases. In Valleyfield about twenty-five entrepreneurs kept workmen busy at this job, for which they were paid ten cents a bottle. The boss made from three to five dollars profit on a case, which Americans sometimes circumvented by paying workmen twenty-five cents a bottle to gather loads for them directly.

Other bootleggers preferred to conduct the entire operation themselves and save the expense of a middleman. For instance, a carload of four men might start north from Rouses Point carrying an assortment of different coats and hats. They visited the liquor stores of St. John, and each purchased his allowed bottle. After donning different garb, they made additional trips to each store. They then moved on to Chambly and then Montreal, where there were sixty-seven stores. Long before they had exhausted the stores they had all the liquor they could get into their car, at official government prices and of the specific brands they wanted. Clerks in the stores knew what was going on, but they were obeying the letter of the law and rarely tried to interrupt a sale. The Quebec Liquor Commission, for its part, obligingly opened stores where the new traffic seemed to warrant it. Early in the Prohibition era the two Valleyfield stores each averaged $200 in daily sales, but by 1923 each manager considered it a poor day that he did not sell $10,000 worth of whiskey.

For relaxation bootleggers maintained camps, at least during the summer months. The one that served the Malone area was at a remote spot in the northern Adirondacks. The one for the Mooers-Champlain-Rouses Point fraternity was located at Rochester Point on Lake Champlain south of Rouses Point. Here the men enjoyed good food prepared by local women employed for housekeeping duties. Each weekend prostitutes were brought from Montreal, and nudist bathing, plenty of liquor, and other pleasures helped to ease the tensions created by the smugglers' trade. The camp also served as a depot for liquor brought by rowboat from Canada and later reshipped in power boats.

Despite the many conditions that worked in his

favor, the bootlegger knew that he was only one step from a stretch in jail, although this was a part of the fascination. He was aware of the danger to his life from gunfire and high-speed driving. If captured, he could expect the penitentiary. If he was challenged but managed to escape, he faced the loss of his car and its contents. Gaston Monette recalls that the dangers he experienced were "so close they are still almost scratching my back."

The narrow, crooked dirt roads of the day often denied the smuggler the speed of which his car was capable, although this factor worked equally against troopers and patrolmen. The sheer distances involved in the liquor traffic added to its complexities. On the map Plattsburgh looked like a short run from the border, but the routes were full of pitfalls. The trip to Glens Falls was 140 miles, to Albany 195 miles, while New York City, the most profitable market, was 350 miles away. Aside from dangers from "the law," the trip was both monotonous and fatiguing. Sam Racicot and Roy Ashline wrecked their car on a trip back from New York when Sam, who was driving, fell asleep.

Car trouble brought many smugglers to grief because all disabled cars attracted attention. Rumrunners were plagued with flat tires, but broken springs and motor failures also took their toll. Gunfire caused breakdowns as well. A patrolman's shots into a gas tank, tires, or radiator usually forced a bootlegger to abandon his car, although some managed sensational escapes on flat tires or with a drained radiator. A rumrunner with a mechanical breakdown could get help by a telephone call to his buddies, but on the party lines of the day he might be overheard and reported. So some preferred to hike to the nearest garage. Billy

Colerich once walked a mile for help after the breakdown of his Model T Ford containing a load of beer. On his return he took the precaution of approaching through the woods, only to see customs officers about to seize his car. He escaped and hitchhiked back to Plattsburgh. The wary ones who had breakdowns learned to conceal their loads in the woods before they went for help. William Riley of Newark, New Jersey, lacked any opportunity of getting away. In his beer-laden truck he broke through the planks of a bridge south of Mooers. Only the steel girders prevented him from plunging into the river.

The passage of the Jones Act caused temporary consternation among drinkers and bootleggers alike, and prices of liquor doubled in most American cities. Violation of the Prohibition law had now become a felony. Prior to this, a rumrunner who deserted his car was thought to be cowardly; youthful bootleggers were considered novices until they had been caught at least once. Under the new law patrolmen made fewer arrests because the harsh penalties encouraged wholesale desertions of loads, with the smugglers running for the woods in greater numbers.

Potentially more dangerous than any of their other difficulties were the consequences of bootleggers falling out among themselves. In its most innocent form this meant giving tips against a rival or stealing his stored stocks. More serious was the arson practiced by one faction to intimidate its rivals. An outbreak of fires occurred in Mooers in 1931, which was stopped only when two men confessed to setting fire to a house which had served as a wholesale and retail liquor dispensary.

Arson was allegedly the cause of a fire in Champlain involving rivalry within a family. At that time Alex Bodette, a part-time bootlegger, was employed on Hugh McLellan's farm, according to his son, Charles (Woody) McLellan. Alex had a quantity of liquor stored in his own cellar, and his son Norman wanted to get his hands on it. The version of the day was that Norman set fire to the barn near McLellan's house, knowing that his father would go to the aid of his employer. During the excitement Norman raided his father's stock and got away with a valuable load of liquor. Sometime later Mr. McLellan was walking on the streets of Plattsburgh with Judge Booth when Norman Bodette drove by in an empty booze car and yelled at the top of his lungs: "Hi, Mr. McLellan, don't you wish you were a bootlegger and travel in a big car like I am?"

The bitterest rivalry that bootleggers had to deal with was the hijacking of loads in transit. This might occur on the streets of Plattsburgh, as when two hijackers took over a horse-drawn load of hay, the hay serving to conceal thirty bags of Canadian ale. More often this was a tactic used in the countryside, especially at night. The hijackers typically wore caps like those used by customs officers. Standing beside the road, they motioned a bootlegger to stop and if necessary fired a warning shot into the air. Bootleggers rarely paused to argue, never being sure that customs officers were not really challenging them, and they took to the woods. Numerous robberies were conducted in this manner, such as the capture in one operation of a Buick, a Hudson, and fifty-five bags of Canadian ale at the Creek bridge just north of Plattsburgh.

For the most part northern New York was

spared the gang warfare that scarred the metropolitan areas during the twenties and early thirties. The so-called Yancey gang moved into the area and although tough, was willing to live and let live with the other bootleggers. When an even tougher gang from New York moved in, however, the Yancey gang opposed them, and eventually the two groups shot it out at the Meridian Hotel. Although only whispered at the time, it was presumed that two members of the new gang were killed and the rest scattered, never to return. The bodies were supposed to have been bound in chains and dumped into Lake Champlain near the railroad bridge.

If a bootlegger could stay out of jail and avoid the other pitfalls of his profession, he might make a great deal of money. Yet the concensus of opinion among the participants is that only a few held onto their money. It seems to have been "easy come, easy go" for most of them. A few substantial businessmen remain in the county who used the profits of rumrunning to start a legitimate enterprise. Farmers who rented their facilities were sometimes able to expand their farms and improve their buildings, but the majority of bootleggers seem to have dissipated their earnings on a succession of expensive cars, necessary to their trade, and on good clothes, women, and other dazzling objects so tempting to the possessor of sudden wealth. Says Keysor, "They bought the most expensive suits and they lived high, they had a good time."

Life of a Border Officer

Consumed liquor is all we let go through. Some of the strongest breaths the world has known pass through here. I am often glad that we use an electric torch instead of an oil lamp in making our night searches, because there might be serious explosions if a naked flame ran afoul of the exhalations of the tourists.

Anonymous Rouses Point Patrolman

OFFICERS ALONG the Canadian border when Prohibition arrived must have felt like draftees in a peacetime army when war broke out: they suddenly found themselves faced with a battle of wit and endurance. They were sometimes captivated by the excitement of the chase, but more often their exuberance was tempered by the stark fact that the way they were making a living was both strenuous and dangerous.

Robert Halstead, customs inspector at Rouses Point, recalls that "we had a lot of fun in those days. But when you are younger, you do things that you look back on with horror as you advance in years." Mrs. Henry Thwaits of Au Sable Forks, then wife of a customs patrolman, declares that she could never live through the Prohibition period again. Although she had two small children and held a teaching position, she also helped her husband with his reports. Aggravating her gnawing fear that he might not come home uninjured were the anonymous letters threatening that she would never see him again if he didn't resign, and naming a deadline.

The training of professional patrolmen and troopers included practice in running, and normally the younger ones could outdistance a fleeing smuggler. It also included learning to handle firearms, which they were authorized to use as was any other law-enforcement officer. If he was inexperienced when he entered the service, a recruit quickly had to acquire some special skills for his lively trade. Among these were coolness under pressure and the exercise of good judgment. Should he, for example, search a grandmotherly-looking woman, investigate a hearse, or arrest an important public figure or a clergyman? Was he justified sometimes in looking the other way? Those who became successful at detecting smugglers soon learned to recognize the "friendly conversationalist," the "winker" of the regular-guy variety, and the "don't-you-dare-put-your-hands-on-me" type.

He also had to develop a sixth sense for deciding which vehicles to search and which travelers to challenge. Even if he found contraband, he had to decide how to handle the situation. Robert Halstead remembers four clergymen driving up to the customs house in Rouses Point. The two in the rumble seat got out, and he found that their seat was cases of beer. Onlookers were sure that the men were not real men of the cloth, but Halstead was satisfied that they were genuine so he merely seized the beer and fined them two dollars a bottle. He did not seize the car, although he could have.

Female smugglers were always a special source

The U.S. Customs Officers and brokers of the F. W. Myers brokerage firm in Rouses Point, N.Y., June 1931. Among those interviewed by the author were Walter Connelly and Jack Ross (first row, first and second from left), Robert Halstead and Ralph Chilton (second row, third and fourth from left), and Roy Delano (third row, fifth from left).

of bewilderment. When an officer became suspicious, his only recourse was to summon his wife, as did John O'Hara at Mooers, or some good-natured woman in the vicinity, to search the female traveler. This work, however, carried no remuneration until 1929. During the heavy tourist season Geraldine Laundrie was appointed to the Rouses Point customs house by the collector of customs at Ogdensburg. In her three months of duty she removed 670 bottles of liquor from the persons of female tourists arriving from Canada and collected fines of $3,050. This was the first border port in the country where a woman inspector was on regular duty. So successful was the experiment that the practice was duplicated elsewhere, and Laundrie herself was back at Rouses Point the next year.

Officers were always considered on duty, regardless of the time or place. A patrolman once drove his wife to Malone on a pleasure trip. At a crossroads he saw three heavily-loaded cars approaching from the north. Finding the bait irresistible, he attempted to stop them. Two of the drivers abandoned their vehicles and ran into the woods while the other turned and raced back toward Canada. There being no telephone nearby with which to summon help, the patrolman asked his wife to drive one of the cars, a Cadillac containing about twenty-five cases of choice liquors, back to Chateaugay. It is not known whether she enjoyed the adventure—her car was a prime target for recapture, and she had to cross a shaky bridge just west of the village.

When Prohibition went into effect the Canadian border was guarded by approximately the same forces that had operated there previously—the Immigration Service and the Customs Patrol. Congress later created the Immigration Border Patrol to help with the enforcement of all federal laws. Consequently, after 1924 the Border Patrol and Customs Patrol bore the brunt of the federal effort to enforce Prohibition at the border.

The Customs Patrol was an arm of the Customs Service, organized solely to watch for violations of the customs laws, one of which forbade the importation of any goods that were illegal in the United States. The Volstead Act complicated the work of enforcement by outlawing all beverages containing more than one-half of one percent alcohol. Although the Customs Patrol continued to watch for the smuggling of undeclared articles such as furs, jewels, and narcotics, Prohibition usurped most of its energies for nearly fourteen years. Smugglers usually dealt in only one commodity, but some handled another for "insurance." Officers soon discovered that some smugglers with a minor sideline would, if caught, admit to a lesser offense in the hopes that a more important violation would not be detected. If pressed, a smuggler might admit to the possession of two bottles of beer (fine $4), hoping to head off further inspection that might reveal five bottles of liquor (fine $25).

The State Police were organized to enforce motor vehicle and other state laws. During the two-year life of the Mullan-Gage Act, they added Prohibition enforcement to their assignments. But even without state Prohibition, smuggling activities so often involved the breaking of some state law that the police were constantly concerned with the bootlegger. He might be speeding, disregarding traffic signs, driving without a license, plates, or lights, or even laying a smoke screen. If he was caught by the State Police and found carrying intoxicating beverages, he was held under the state Prohibition law or, after its repeal, under the federal law, and turned over to federal authorities. Thus the police furnished considerable help in the capture of bootleggers; they went so far as to cooperate with the other agencies in setting up roadblocks and conducting raids. The headquarters of Troop B was located in Malone, and from there the officers patrolled the whole northern border, but like the other services they were grossly understaffed for the magnitude of their job—there were only sixteen of them for the northern New York border in 1923, and their numbers were not substantially increased in subsequent years.

Other agencies for law enforcement included the sheriff's department (especially while New York had its own Prohibition law) and the city police of Plattsburgh, where repeated raids failed to end the retailing of liquor. The Military Police at the Plattsburgh Barracks cooperated with the city police in numerous raids aimed at protecting the soldiers from the evils of alcohol. Areas adjacent to the barracks—United States Avenue and Elizabeth and Charlotte streets—became centers of the liquor trade, just as they had previously contained many of the town's saloons.

Efforts to dry up this area under local Prohibition had been made even before the national law became effective. During World War I military authorities were particularly concerned because of the shell-shocked soldiers who were receiving treatment and for whom alcohol in any form was dangerous, especially the concoctions that were available at the time. Both then and later the provost marshal accompanied civil officers in raids on speakeasies, particularly in the

U.S. Custom House. Rouses Point N.Y.

The customs house in Rouses Point, N.Y. Almost a mile from the border, the customs offices occupied the entire second floor, and travelers were supposed to stop here to report. A customs house was later built at the border.

vicinity of the barracks, but the soldiers refused to be "insulated," and when necessary they made trips to Canada for their beer and liquor.

On the border between Clinton County and the province of Quebec, the small forces in the Border Patrol, Customs Patrol, and State Police guarded a frontier thirty-three miles long. Almost twenty roads crossed into Canada, to say nothing of the paths through fields and woods. Three important customs stations were located on the main routes into New York State—Rouses Point, Champlain, and Mooers. In all three places the customs house was not at the border, as it is now, but a mile or more to the south, within the villages. All traffic was supposed to stop for inspection, and most of the travelers and petty smugglers did so because they did not know the alternatives. A few of the commercial smugglers did also, if they thought their load was safely concealed. But most of the large-scale smugglers used the side roads except at night, when the customs house was closed. The busiest station was at Rouses Point, which was on the only paved road into Canada, the "Rum Trail" between Albany and Montreal.

However, patrols were needed on the many roads other than the three main ones. Officers soon discovered certain bottlenecks where they could prepare roadblocks at night. One was in Miner's Woods on Route 9 north of Chazy where the high fences on both sides of the road made escape difficult for rumrunners who abandoned their cars. Another was a two-mile stretch of woods on top of Rand Hill. Smugglers were sometimes vulnerable in the slow traffic of Plattsburgh. There were other traps south of the city, the most famous being the Poke-O'-Moonshine area south of Keeseville, where steep grades and crooked roads forced rumrunners to slow down.

Since smugglers were making generous use of the railroad, customs and immigration officers had to keep a special watch over the Delaware and Hudson line at Rouses Point. Individual travelers used passenger trains for smuggling, but the commercial smugglers learned to use the freight car with great profit and minimum risk, since they did not need to be present with the shipment. Consequently, officials had to open and examine every freight car, empty or loaded, on a long train. If they suspected false ends to the car, they had at great effort to unload the legitimate part of the contents. This task usually resulted from a suspicious odor, leaking beverages, or a tip, although officers acquired great skill in spotting foreshortened cars on their own. The many clever methods of concealment made detection difficult, yet the officers were acutely aware of the urgency of their work, for if a freight car of contraband was allowed through Rouses Point it probably would not be detected on its long journey south unless it needed repairs.

Customs and immigration officers also had to try to stem the flow of liquor on Lake Champlain. This waterway, with outlets at each end, led from Canada to the Hudson River and was the scene of considerable smuggling. Until 1922 customs officers had no boat with which to patrol or pursue. They had to be satisfied with the capture of vessels which required the railroad bridge to be opened or which stopped at customs at Rouses Point, as all craft were supposed to. The slow-moving boats invariably did so, but the fast ones preferred to make a dash up the open lake. In 1922 the first government boat was put into operation, and six agents started to patrol the lake. The craft had a speed of thirty-five miles an hour, which was sufficient to overtake most of the other boats of the day. Beginning in 1924 the force was slowly expanded; eventually the Coast Guard took over enforcement activities on the lake.

Assignment to duty at a customs house meant checking all suspicious-looking cars and people. Small-time smugglers tried to carry a few bottles for their personal use. Some panicked at the last minute and declared their contraband. In that case, they were not fined, but the liquor was confiscated. Most of them, however, tried concealment, and if liquor was then discovered on their persons, in their cars, or in the luggage of train passengers, the owners lost the liquor and were fined two dollars a bottle for beer and five dollars for liquor. The formal procedure required the traveler to sign an "Assent to Forfeiture and Destruction," surrender the liquor or beer, and deposit an "Offer of Civil Settlement" in cash. Civil settlement was always agreed to at the border because a traveler was not considered a "professional" smuggler, and it saved everybody a trip to court.

Suspicion that a cache of liquor might be concealed beneath the car led officers like John O'Hara at Mooers to get on their backs and crawl under for a look. O'Hara became disgusted with this procedure and arranged mirrors to save himself the trouble. In time mirrors and lights became standard equipment at all customs stations along the border, simply because one officer didn't want to soil his shirt.

Border officers might be assigned to duty along the lakeshore, in the railroad yards, at the customs house, or along the numerous roads. They might be required for night patrol and were periodically detailed to take part in raids on stills, loading stations, and speakeasies, sometimes as far away as Albany. There was always less likelihood of "leaks" about a proposed raid when it was conducted by federal officers rather than by local officials.

When an officer made an arrest, he was required to arraign his prisoner before the United States commissioner in Plattsburgh. If the commissioner bound the prisoner over for a grand jury, the case went before the United States District Court for the Northern District of New York. The arresting officer was supposed to appear before the grand jury and also at the trial, whether it was held in Albany, Utica, Binghamton, or elsewhere. Failure to appear meant that the case was dismissed. Border patrolmen recall having to make multiple trips to a single session of federal court. When several officers were away at the same time, the border was relatively undefended, and bootleggers soon learned to make the most of these periodic opportunities.

One of the more onerous duties of patrolmen was the disposition of captured liquor. Seizures at a customs station might average only two or three bottles per car, but the searching of hundreds of cars daily might yield thousands of gallons in a week. Jack Ross, former customs officer at Rouses Point, recalls that for a while all this liquid was poured down the toilet at the customs house. But eventually the owner of the building, John Myers, president of the F. W. Myers firm of customs brokers, put his foot down because the liquor was making the pipes leak. In fairness to its quality, Ross points out, the liquor did not eat through the metal of the pipes, but rather seeped through the packed joints.

During the course of a seizure that might lead to

Thomas Duncan destroying seized liquor at the dump opposite the Catholic Church in Rouses Point, N.Y.

U.S. Marshal destroying liquor before a crowd of interested citizens at the dump in Rouses Point, N.Y.

a court case, an officer always took care to preserve some of the stock as evidence. The rest was normally stored at the customs house or in rented facilities. From time to time, orders came from higher authority to destroy the stored goods. When no court case was likely, as was usual with seizures of freight cars, the stock was destroyed immediately. Ralph J. Chilton of Rouses Point, then a customs appraiser, recalls that in the early years liquor was destroyed by breaking bottles on an iron rail opposite the Catholic church. What is now a park was once deeply covered with broken glass. The largest destruction in which he per-

69

sonally was involved was a freight carload of 500 cases of champagne.

In Plattsburgh liquor was usually stored in the basement or on the third floor of the federal building. It was generally believed at the time that the janitors were able to keep themselves supplied with a bottle now and then. On one occasion, when removal was ordered from the third floor, the few officers detailed to the heavy work resorted to throwing the liquor out of the window. Ten thousand bottles of beer and twenty-five hundred bottles of choice wines, liquors, and champagne were pitched to the ground. For a time, the streets of Plattsburgh literally ran with alcohol. On other occasions the liquor was poured, bottle by bottle, down the sewer in Plattsburgh, or broken at the dump at the mouth of the Saranac River.

Once started, the task of destruction had to be carried through to completion or else the unbroken bottles had to be guarded all night. Walter Connelly, a customs officer at Rouses Point, remembers guarding seized freight cars that had not yet been unloaded. Guard duty consisted of walking around the car every half hour all night. He also recalls working at the dump until ten o'clock one night in a snowstorm in order to finish a job.

Large-scale destruction was superintended by a United States marshal or a deputy marshal, who had specific orders from Washington. Deputy Marshal George W. Andress was usually involved in such activities along the northern border. In July 1922, he broke 3,500 bottles of liquor and 400 of beer at Rouses Point, without doing much to relieve the storage problem. There, at Plattsburgh and Malone he supervised

Sale at Rouses Point by U.S. Marshal of cars and other equipment seized during the rumrunning days.

the destruction of 40,500 bottles during the week of April 16, 1923. The Canadian value of the goods was $200,000, the American, $500,000. In September 1924, he disposed of 93,960 bottles of ale at Rouses Point. This stock had been seized on the barge *E. Daneau*. It was destroyed by being towed to the end of the breakwater and broken bottle by bottle. Citizens of the area wondered, if this practice was continued, what would happen to the fish of Lake Champlain.

71

They might well have wondered what would happen to the bottom of the lake.

Auctions were also directed by Marshal Andress. Everything seized from a rumrunner except his liquor was sold periodically to the highest bidder and the proceeds went to the federal treasury. The most valuable commodity was automobiles, but the list also included boats, sleighs, horses, motorcycles, bicycles, and snowshoes. Sometimes twenty-five or thirty cars would be auctioned in a month. At one Rouses Point auction, nine cars brought $2,986. The highest price was $1,600 for a Cadillac, the lowest $51 for a Ford roadster. Graphic new words entered the vocabulary as rumrunners' cars were referred to as "hootchmobiles," "boozemobiles," and "beermobiles." Smugglers or their agents sometimes repurchased cars at the auctions. But the government kept some of the best of them for the patrolmen, gradually replacing the cheaper, lighter cars. Ralph Chilton quotes an old service tradition that the Packard touring car made the quickest getaway, but that the Cadillac was better in tough going—it settled down and handled better on curves and at high speeds. Both models were capable of top speeds while fully loaded, with specially built springs to sustain the load.

In the month of October 1921, thirty cars valued at between $40,000 and $50,000 were seized along the northern border. For the entire year, at Rouses Point alone, seizures included 117 autos, 18 horses and rigs, and approximately 2,000 cases of liquor. If the quantities of destroyed or auctioned goods seem incredibly large, they become more understandable after a glance at the total traffic at the border.

This photo of Overton's Corners Border Station shows the volume of traffic that had to be inspected. This station was on the King Edward Highway (then Route 9, now 9B or 223), which was the only surfaced road into Canada at that time.

During the 1920s, thanks to prosperity and the increase in car ownership, traffic increased greatly, as did the seizures. The sheer numbers of cars and travelers, each of them potentially engaged in smuggling, made a mockery of the small forces available to enforce the law.

In April 1929, a total of 2,965 cars entered the

country at Rouses Point carrying 8,837 persons, along with 213 passenger trains with 10,171 persons, all of which had to be inspected. Mail, express, and baggage packages totaled 52,159 items, while 10,265 freight cars vastly multiplied the task. In November 23,915 passengers entered the country by car and 11,753 by train. For the entire year, almost one million persons passed through the village by car or train. Fines totaled more than $22,000, while arrests led to dozens of court cases from this port of entry alone. Seizures included liquor, wine, beer, alcohol, mash, home brew, and cider, all in large quantities.

The strenuous, sometimes exciting, and often dangerous workday of the patrolmen was nine hours, recalls Philip Auer, formerly of the Border Patrol. But, he adds, "hardly a day of it we didn't work twelve, fifteen, or eighteen hours a day." After he had worked at Rouses Point for two months, he asked for a day off and Chief Patrol Inspector Bonanzi said, "A day off? I never heard of such a thing!" Auer recalls that later the officers did get a day off occasionally. Connelly remembers the long days on the hot pavement and the long nights of destroying liquor or of standing guard after which he was still expected to report for duty at eight o'clock in the morning.

In the early twenties, the pay for members of the border and customs patrols was $1,680 a year, and out of this they had to provide their own uniforms. In time this was raised to $1,860, and Robert Halstead remembers several men of twenty-five years service who were raised from $1,800 to the new maximum. In 1927 the pay was increased to $2,000 and by 1930 to

$2,100. In addition to long hours and low pay, customs officers were so poorly equipped at the start that they sometimes hired taxis to make their night patrols. Not until the establishment of the Border Patrol in 1924 were specially trained officers and good equipment available.

At the beginning of the Prohibition era, the State Police were paid $900 a year and maintenance. The highest they could get was $1,270 after eight years of service, but no one qualified for that much because the service was so young. In 1924 the maximum pay was raised to $1,300. If they married, they were likely to be dismissed or transferred repeatedly from station to station, as it was thought a married man would have to divide his attentions between work and family.

Under the circumstances, the record of integrity of the officers on the border was remarkable. Their own pay was a pittance compared with the profits of bootlegging. Most of them, at one time or another, were approached by bootleggers who sought to buy their help or protection. Auer recalls being asked on various occasions, "Why don't you wise up and make some money?" " 'Listen, you goddam monkeys,' I says, 'if I could make $50,000 a night I'd take it probably and resign tomorrow,' but I knew that the minute you took a nickel from any of these guys you were behind the eight-ball right off." One Rouses Point customs officer reported an offer of $15,000 to clear certain cars. Contrary to the opinion of the day, border officers were generally not corruptible, yet since many of them did not like the laws they were supposed to enforce, they were not all as dedicated as the respected Hamilton McCrea, who was reputed to be willing to arrest his own father if necessary.

Some did not hesitate to withhold a bottle or two from a seizure. Others had personal weaknesses that the bootleggers learned to exploit. One officer was known to be fond of women, and there was no problem finding a female who would decoy him behind the shed while the loads of liquor rolled through unhindered. Another officer, not popular among his colleagues, was a heavy drinker. One night he developed a toothache and at one o'clock in the morning roused a Plattsburgh dentist. The officer decided that he needed a drink before the dentist pulled his tooth, and he took a bottle into the office. The dentist thought that a drink was what he needed also, and what with one drink and then another they both got high. When the officer, having forgotten his toothache, got up to take an unsteady leave, the dentist suddenly recalled the bad tooth. Getting the officer into the chair, he extracted nine teeth before his enthusiasm began to wane. The officer's mouth was so badly lacerated that he needed two weeks for repairs at the hospital.

Off-duty officers had the same human appetites as civilians. Some were good customers at Mrs. Brunck's restaurant and night spot in Rouses Point. One of them had an affair with her twenty-year-old daughter which produced a threat of divorce from his wife. Officers were sometimes weekend guests at the bootleggers' summer camp on Rochester Point, where relaxation was provided by wine and women.

Officers occasionally were suspended or dismissed. In 1925 fifteen agents in northern New York were quietly dropped "for the good of the service." No names or charges were publicized, but the action was rumored to be part of a larger movement to put the service on its toes. In 1929 an officer at Champlain was suspended for "conduct unbecoming an officer," and another at Rouses Point for "dereliction of duty." Some lost their jobs when they were put under civil service to combat political influence in the making of appointments. Not all of them could pass the civil service examination.

Border officers sometimes left their jobs and went into bootlegging. When they did so, they were likely to be extraordinarily tough and skillful, for they knew all the routes and tricks of the trade from the inside. Ralph Hackmeister, until 1922 known as "the terror of rumrunners" for his harsh enforcement of the law, resigned from the Customs Patrol. The next year he was arrested and charged with rumrunning, but his case was dismissed for lack of evidence. Edward Cronk, formerly of Troop B at Malone, was arrested and charged with rumrunning and with hijacking a load of liquor. He was convicted and sent to jail, and troopers said Cronk was one of the most desperate rumrunners they had seen. When he left the force he boasted that he would go into the rum game and that no one in the United States would catch him. Floyd Cool was another ex-trooper who turned bootlegger. Captured in Champlain in 1931 and handcuffed to a fellow captive, he and his partner escaped into Canada. Several months later he was identified in an Albany hospital where he was receiving treatment for a wound containing glass. He received a suspended sentence to the federal penitentiary in Atlanta, Georgia, and was put on four years probation provided he stayed out of the North Country.

The most sensational case involving illegal acts of border officers while they were still in the service occurred in 1930, when four patrolmen at Mooers and fourteen civilians of Mooers and Sciota were indicted on charges of conspiracy and bribery in a smuggling ring. Most of them were convicted in federal court and given jail sentences, large fines, or both. Of the patrolmen, Welden J. Cheatham was fined $2,000 and sent to the Atlanta penitentiary for twenty months for conspiracy and bribery. For the same offences, Charles Cooligan received fourteen months and Colin Morris, one year and a day. But the fourth officer, Francis Coveney, was fined $2,000 and sentenced to Atlanta for three terms of two years each, to be served concurrently. Paroled nine months before the completion of the sentence, he apparently returned to northern New York to engage in smuggling. Arrested and held temporarily at the Mooers customs house, he escaped and led federal, county, and city officers on a wild chase until he was recaptured in Plattsburgh. He had forfeited his parole from his previous sentence and now, with several new charges against him, was back in the penitentiary to stay for awhile.

Every border agent had to work out his own procedures for dealing with a fast-moving situation. When an officer could not stop a smuggler he was chasing by getting ahead of him, he tried shooting, either at the tires or gas tank of the smuggler's car. If, as often happened, the bootlegger jumped from his car and ran for the woods, the pursuing officer was supposed to fire one shot in the air and order a halt. Auer

78

decided early not to shoot again. If the man continued to run, as he usually did, the officer had to do the best he could on foot. In Auer's case, this was usually the end of the matter for he was not fast on his feet and his man often got away. Other officers were more nimble and executed some remarkable captures over rough terrain at night.

A source of hostility to patrolmen and troopers was a charge of indiscriminate use of fists and firearms. Every incident made the headlines. Editorials were written and, ultimately, questions were asked in Congress. As early as 1921, a trooper from Company B was accused of assaulting his handcuffed prisoners.

But it was the shootings that caused the furor. In their zeal to stop a speeding car, some officers apparently fired excessively and instead of hitting tires or gas tanks, sometimes riddled the upper part of the car. Likewise, a smuggler fleeing on foot might find bullets raining around him. Little was said as long as the occupants of the car or the running man were not hit, but when they were a hue and cry was raised about the wisdom of officers being armed. "Shot by Immigration Officers" made an ugly headline. Since violations of the Prohibition law were at first only misdemeanors, injury or death seemed too high a price to pay for enforcement of the law. As the law itself became more unpopular, the outcry became sharper.

If no one pressed charges, the excitement died down. When an aggrieved person did bring charges, however, a border agent might be called into a local court for questioning, as was Hamilton McCrea in 1924. If local officials were determined to press a case, federal authorities stepped in and transferred it to federal court. There the officer was tried under federal law, and if he was exonerated for having merely tried to do his duty, cries of "whitewash" were often heard.

In a shooting where the facts were clear, there was disposition in all courts to dismiss the charges and call the situation regrettable but understandable, considering that border officers were often dealing with armed violators of the law. But when there was conflicting testimony, when death resulted from being run over by an officer's car, or when there was a suspicion of promiscuous shooting, the officer might be in for trouble. This was the situation Trooper Ralph Travis faced for wounding Guy Martin near Ingraham and running down his partner, Louis Belisar, when he tried to jump out of the fleeing car. The case against Travis became more serious when Martin died and a soft lead bullet was taken from his lung.

Samuel Dickson was charged with first-degree murder in Plattsburgh city court for killing an alleged bootlegger, Otto Eske, the "Big Swede," in 1925. Witnesses in Cooperville testified that Dickson took deliberate aim at Eske. The case was remanded to federal court, where it was postponed several times and eventually dropped. Even before the end of the month, Dickson was free on bond and back on duty at Rouses Point. Two years later Dickson was again in local court, charged with "discharging firearms in a public place." He was supposed to have shot at the separate cars containing Lieutenant Rafael Salzman and Captain E. S. Dollarhide of the Twenty-sixth Infantry, stationed at Plattsburgh. Although no injury resulted, federal court again intervened.

Shootings continued to disturb the peace of the

countryside and led the *Plattsburgh Republican* to condemn the wild-west tactics of border patrolmen. The case that really rocked the North Country, however, was the death in 1929 of Arthur Gordon on the road between Perrys Mills and Mooers. It was the climax of six shootings in the preceding ten days, none of them fatal. Violation of the Jones Act made violation of the Prohibition laws a felony, and state law allowed a felon to be shot if he tried to escape; consequently, District Attorney B. Loyal O'Connell at first thought there was nothing he could do, although he pressed an investigation. But some disturbing questions began to emerge. Just how had Gordon died? Conflicting evidence was given on this point, the officers remaining silent. Why had the officers who brought the body to the hospital disappeared without making a report?

The district attorney appealed to Seymour Lowman, assistant secretary of the Treasury, to cooperate in getting the customs officers into court. Lowman suggested that the men be subpoenaed in the usual manner. President Hoover was quoted as deploring the border shootings but asked the border communities to "help the treasury in the systematic war that is being carried on by international criminals against the laws of the United States." Reports of the shooting reached the floor of Congress, where wets and drys denounced or upheld the enforcement authorities according to their own opinions about Prohibition.

The suspected officers eventually were brought into the coroner's court of Dr. Edwin Sartwell, where they refused to incriminate themselves. Collector Tulloch, however, had already reported that those responsible for the death were officers Francis L.

Coveney and Weldon J. Cheatham, the latter of whom had stumbled and accidentally fired his revolver. These were two of the men who, a year later, would be convicted of conspiracy and bribery. Cheatham was charged with second-degree manslaughter and bound over to the grand jury under $7,500 bail, but, the jury failed to return an indictment, and the charge was consequently dismissed.

If members of the Customs Patrol, Border Patrol, and the State Police managed to do their jobs in spite of these many demands on their time and skill, they faced numerous other harrassments and pitfalls. They were assumed by bootleggers to be ignorant or greedy or both: "A good many very smart people were of the opinion that customs officers didn't know too much at times, and they would try, just to be smart," recalls Robert Halstead. Any trick was fair play if it served to outwit these "misguided" guardians of the law. The Elks Club once had a clambake just over the border which was watched, according to Robert C. Booth, then city judge, by officers on the American side who, when they returned to their cars, found sand in their gas tanks!

They were also frustrated by the knowledge that only a small percentage of contraband was being stopped—anywhere from 5–20 percent was the estimate. Others had the gnawing conviction that Prohibition was not right—"a bum law," Philip Auer called it. Some wasted their energies on false pursuits, as did State Trooper Mitchell LaFave who followed Ross Sanger and a heavy load of potatoes out of Ingraham; or Hamilton McCrea and Captain Orr, both armed, who stalked each other on foot in the dark; only a mutual scrutiny of their credentials disclosed that each had apprehended the other. Neither one boasted of this exploit but word got around anyway, and they were happily reminded of it by their colleagues.

Several officers were injured or killed in the line of duty. Pat Goodrow, a customs officer, landed in the hospital with bullet wounds in both legs after a shooting fray north of Rouses Point. Although the fleeing car left a trail of leaking whiskey as far as Chazy, the bootleggers evaded their pursuers and got away. On another occasion Ansell Molleur of Chazy, a former customs officer who was hired to drive for other agents, was killed when they tried to capture beer runners who had deserted their car on the Turnpike near Altona. But the misfortunes of enforcement officers caused far fewer headlines and controversies than resulted when rumrunners were the victims. This was true despite the well-known acts of violence practiced repeatedly by bootleggers.

The immediate custody of a seizure was often a perplexing problem. Customs Officer Henry Thwaits once had a complicated problem on his hands. Driving north on Route 22 one night, he had reached the White Pine Tearoom near Beekmantown when he spotted a line of cars approaching. In an effort to back across the road he got stuck in the ditch. He jumped out and shot into the air over the approaching vehicles, whereupon they were run into the ditch or the fence, the drivers all fleeing and leaving six abandoned cars. Thwaits locked the cars and went into the tearoom at one o'clock in the morning to call for help. At the telephone he was challenged by a frightened woman pointing a shaking automatic pistol at him. After satisfying her of his identity, he completed the call and eventually received reinforcements. It is unlikely that the bootleggers knew Thwaits was alone, or they would have tried to rush him and recapture their cars. As it was, he effected the seizure, single-handedly, of six cars loaded with liquor, plus another whose driver blundered into the area while he and his assistants were sorting out the situation.

Herman Stevenson of the Mooers station solved a similar problem in a different way, as Elmer Caron tells it. A quarter of a mile north of Route 11, on the Churubusco road, Stevenson found himself in uneasy control of three carloads of liquor whose drivers had sought refuge behind a stone wall. With no telephone on the Caron farm, Stevenson moved all three cars by successively driving the rear car around in front of the others. Slowly he inched them all down to Route 11, where he found a farmer who let him use a telephone, but the townspeople never forgave the farmer for being so helpful. In fact, says Caron, on both sides of the border barns belonging to informers or those who cooperated with patrolmen were sometimes burned.

Officers consequently learned that they could expect little help in the countryside because so many of the citizens were either unsympathetic with the law, fearful of reprisals, or determined not to get a smuggler-neighbor into trouble. Sometimes private citizens even tried to interfere with the processes of seizure and arrest, as Henry Thwaits discovered after a chase from Keeseville to Au Sable Forks. At the edge of the Forks, the fleeing driver jumped and tried to escape, but the river stopped him and Thwaits caught him after firing into the air. The neighbors however, (from his own home town) tried to help the prisoner escape, and Thwaits had to use handcuffs to hold him.

Not everything was stacked against a patrolman, however. There *were* tipsters and informers, often anonymous, whose information led to significant seizures. Information might come from a rival bootlegger, from a law-abiding citizen, or from a homeowner outraged at the goings-on next door. The latter source accounted for many of the raids on speakeasies in Plattsburgh, for the chief of police let it be known repeatedly that he would act upon any complaints he received. Other tips led to captures on the roads and railroads at the border. Officers made every effort to conceal the source of their information, so that it would be continued.

The weather was also sometimes on the side of the law. Lake Champlain was normally frozen three months of the year, and rumrunning boats were consequently out of commission. Northern winters often closed the roads into Canada for weeks on end, and at the beginning of the Prohibition era when there was little snow removal on any roads bootleggers were forced to use sleighs and snowshoes. When systematic snowplowing of the main roads was inaugurated during the winter of 1923–24, patrolmen still had the advantage that none of the back roads or short cuts would be open, and they could thus patrol the few open routes with more concentration. Even after a start was made to keep a few roads open, high winds often created great drifts as soon as the plow had passed.

The work of a border patrolman ranged from the

difficult to the impossible. Most of the officers did the best they could, were usually dogged in their attention to duty, and occasionally brilliant in their daring and inventiveness. They are unsung heroes largely because the law they were charged to enforce was eventually discarded.

Officer Confronts Bootlegger

I always figured that if a man left the car, if he started to run, I'd always fire one shot, and that was in the air, and I'd holler for him to stop. If he didn't stop, that was it. When I see I couldn't catch him, I always figured that there's no man's life worth a load of booze.

Philip Auer of Rouses Point

I lost three cars; I ran away from three cars. Tires stopped one of them. I thought there was no way of getting by a block, so I just slowed the car, jumped out, and let the car keep running, and fortunately at that time they didn't see me get out of the car—they were on the wrong side—and I disappeared. The third time I got out of the car and ran and one of the officers went by and shined his light directly on me and motioned me to squat down, and I squatted down and he walked by me.

Sam Racicot of Rouses Point

DAY AFTER DAY for more than thirteen years showdowns occurred along the border with Canada over the illegal carrying of alcohol across the line. Some of the gentler confrontations are comic, if not ludicrous. Consider the southbound traveler being questioned by Customs Officer Jack Ross. The man insisted he had nothing to declare. Ross said, "What's that in your inner coat pocket?" The man reached in and pulled out a

87

bottle of fine liquor and said, "Who put that there?" Or consider the smuggler who had distributed the contents of a big bottle among five small ones in order to conceal them better. When caught, instead of a flat five-dollar fine he paid five dollars on each bottle, in addition to losing the liquor.

Robert Halstead recalls searching a car at the border without finding any contraband. He then reached into the owner's pocket to see what caused a bulge and instead of the liquor he expected, he found a $300 jade necklace. He asked the traveler why he had not declared it and claimed exemption on part of its value. The traveler blandly stated that "he thought it was a good test of customs efficiency!" When caught, smugglers loudly declaimed their ignorance about how liquor came to be concealed in their cars. Claims like this were of no help because the driver or person in charge of the vehicle was legally responsible for all articles aboard. Passengers had a better chance than drivers when they said that they did not know the driver was carrying liquor, because their claims were difficult to disprove.

Sometimes more strenuous comedy was played out, such as the time a customs officer at Mooers made a capture armed only with a broom. A traveler reported at the station in a snow-covered car and said he had nothing to declare. Suspecting a ruse, the officer grabbed a broom with which to clear the car. He soon discovered that the gas tank had been divided and that part of it contained liquor. The owner started to run, and broom in hand the officer went after him. Both were good runners, but the road was slippery and down went the bootlegger. He regained his feet and for almost forty rods maintained his lead. The officer called after him, "Stop, or I'll hit you." Since his only weapon was the broom, no injury resulted but he caught his man and sent him to the commissioner in Plattsburgh.

Some of the border patrolmen were local people. Howard Curtis remembers one in Mooers who was acquainted with everyone in town, and when the young men started running liquor, he was troubled and decided to use some unorthodox methods to discourage them. One night a youth drove a Model T and a load of whiskey through town. The patrolman recognized the car and knew that it belonged to a hard-working farmer. Jumping into his old Studebaker, he followed the lad, honked his horn, and signalled for him to stop, without result. He then forced his quarry to go so fast that he could not make a sharp turn and drove into a plowed field instead, bringing the chase to a halt. The patrolman shouted, "Irving, it's only two miles home. Walk, and send your father down with a team tomorrow morning to get the car out." So Irving did not go to jail, and he was so badly frightened that he gave up rumrunning.

A male traveler sometimes had a woman with him to provide companionship on his Canadian jaunt or to beguile the officers at the border. Many a woman was expected to conceal liquor on her person. Customs officers soon learned to be suspicious of women as well as men and to call for female help when a body search seemed warranted. Robert Halstead once found a woman with two hot-water bottles of liquor tied under her abdomen. He says it did not smell appetizing when he dumped it, and he doubts that it would have tasted very good. Robert C. Booth tells of a young lieutenant and his wife who bought some sparkling burgundy in Canada and quart flasks to hold it. She hid them in her bloomers where her body heat forced off the caps, bathing her in a red fluid.

If an officer was suspicious of the passengers in a car he asked them to get out, at which point the clink of glass would sometimes betray a smuggler. Walter Connelly remembers a female tourist whom he directed upstairs in the customs house at Rouses Point. She made it only half way before she gave up. She too had liquor concealed in her bloomers! Women were superb amateur smugglers, but most of the professionals were men. The female companion could expect to be abandoned by her male partner when a chase became too hot. Both of them understood that the law would not be as severe on a female passenger as it would on the driver.

Other combinations of passengers were sometimes thought to dispel suspicions at the border. What could be so charming as a happy family out to see the countryside, even if the children were sitting on bags of beer? Given the volume of traffic past a station, such a car might be waved through without question. Or what was so innocent as a father and small son going through customs on a motorcycle? Yet Eli Girard of Montreal and a nine-year-old boy were stopped on the outskirts of Plattsburgh. The boy was riding in the sidecar on two cases of liquor.

Even clerical garb was used to try to bamboozle customs officers. A hearse once drew up near customs in Champlain with a flat tire. Two nuns got out of the vehicle and an officer, listening from within the building, heard one of them say in a bass voice: "Ain't this a hell of a place to have a flat tire!" A search of the hearse revealed that the casket was full of liquor, and of course the "nuns" were wolves in sheep's clothing.

Bootleggers sometimes gave themselves away unwittingly to their pursuers. Animals once betrayed their owners in a winter adventure along the boundary between Clinton and Franklin counties. Smugglers carrying liquor on five two-horse teams lost one of their loads to the Border Patrol. The others counted on drifting snow to cover their tracks as they fled to their camp on Upper Chateaugay Lake. They had barely arrived when the patrolmen drove up with the captured team and seized the rest of their liquor. The smugglers always believed that a stool-pigeon had betrayed them, but the officers assert that they merely gave the horses their heads and a homing instinct did the rest.

Philip Auer once received an unintended tip when he drove up to a Plattsburgh address, with no particular purpose in mind. But when a man hissed urgently to him, "Put your lights out," he decided to look around. He found three cars loaded with beer and two sheds full of the same—he had stumbled on an important transfer station. Henry Thwaits had a similar experience in Keene. One day he was chatting with Moses Fineberg, who lived on top of Spruce Hill. Fineberg, not knowing his visitor, boasted to him about two loaded cars in his barn. When Thwaits showed his badge, Fineberg almost collapsed, but he agreed to cooperate. Thwaits seized the cars and telephoned for drivers. He did not arrest Fineberg because although he was helping the smugglers, he probably could not have been convicted.

Smugglers also gave themselves away by trying to mix rumrunning with the illegal transportation of aliens, sometimes with strange consequences. One evening Auer stopped a car and noticed a number of women besides the driver, who was a man. On being questioned, the man said that the girls were chambermaids from Lake Placid whom he had taken to Canada for a good time. Auer spoke to a couple of the women, but they didn't seem to understand what he was saying, so he got in the car and told the driver to return to Rouses Point. On the way the driver surrendered a couple of bottles of liquor, saying, "We don't want to get into trouble." Auer took the bottles, knowing that if the driver was otherwise in the clear, he could still be charged with possession of liquor. At the station he put the eight women in a separate room and rushed around the building to look in the window. He saw them hastily hiding their passports in their bloomers. A female neighbor was called to search the women, and their passports revealed them to be Finns trying to enter the country illegally.

There was little humor in most of the confrontations between bootlegger and officer, however. Each was engaged in a serious, sometimes desperate, attempt to outwit the other. Liquor was being smuggled into the country by railroad, boat, and highway and each route needed but did not have a small army for proper patrolling.

The most vulnerable of the railroad bootleggers were those who tried to smuggle liquor in person. If detected, they were subject to the same "civil settlement" and fine that prevailed on the highways. They exploited all the natural hiding places the train had to offer, including their personal luggage. Philip Auer once noticed a man boarding the train at Rouses Point who seemed to be having trouble with his suitcase. In reply to questions, the man said it was "just clothes." Auer ordered it opened and discovered twelve quarts of Napoleon cognac, bought in Canada at $25 a bottle. This man was a member of the so-called "suitcase brigade," as were those who used trunks with false sides or bottoms. The station at Rouses Point was a busy place on weekends and during special railroad excursions, when customs officers often required help to remove their haul from a train. Prolonged inspections frequently delayed the departure of trains for New York City.

A customs discovery occasionally was awkward when it involved well-known people. The private railroad car of Geraldine Farrar, a famous singer, was searched at Rouses Point and found to contain forty bottles of choice liquors. It turned up in the piano, the maid's room, and the ventilators. Miss Farrar was in bed and was not charged. Flo Ziegfeld of Follies fame had a similar misfortune. One hundred and six bottles of liquor and 42 quarts of Canadian ale were found in his private car. The car was detached from the train while the stock, worth $3,000 and mostly European in origin, was unloaded. Ziegfeld and two friends paid fines totalling $614 and were allowed to go on their way. Celebrities made the same "civil settlement" that any ordinary tourist did.

Despite the anonymity railroad car smuggling

offered and the ingenuity of the bootleggers, their plots were often detected in the railroad yards at Rouses Point, resulting in huge seizures. Close inspection usually followed the receipt of anonymous tips by telephone or telegraph. Their sources cannot be identified with any certainty, but some probably came from Canadian railroad officials and from rival bootleggers. Seizures also resulted from the tell-tale odor of broken bottles, a car in need of repairs, or an interior whose dimensions aroused suspicions. Walter Connelly recalls once thinking a car looked too short inside, and "I took a bar and we punched the end of the car and out spurted a gush of beer."

When customs officers started weighing freight cars to detect discrepancies between actual and stated weights, smugglers took more care to bill their liquor as material that had a comparable weight and appearance and a plausible-sounding receiver at the other end. Thus a carload of "pulpwood" was consigned to Ticonderoga, where the paper mill was known to consume large quantities of it; a hundred cases of liquor were once discovered on a siding there, concealed under a layer of wood. A load of "waste paper and cardboard boxes" addressed to the International Paper Company at Fort Edward was intercepted at Whitehall and found to contain 6,555 bottles of Frontenac ale. In a load of "lumber" sent to the Special Box Company of Brooklyn Rouses Point officials uncovered liquor which was valued at $100,000 at retail prices. Milk cans from Churubusco were found to contain two quarts of cream and eight gallons of liquor, cans from Mooers had false bottoms, and a shipment of "hay" for a grain and feed dealer in Hudson Falls yielded 5,180 quarts of Molson's ale valued at $3,000.

Customs officers at Rouses Point hold the metal prods which were used to detect contraband concealed beneath hay in a railroad freight car.

Hay and lumber were the most frequently used materials for covering the illegal part of a load. Newsprint (hiding 166 barrels of Carling's), laths (concealing 100 cases of liquor) and various other inexpensive materials were used either to cover the contraband or to block access to the ends of the freight car, where false ends might have been constructed. When seized, the liquor was stored and eventually destroyed, while the hay or other products were auctioned for the benefit of the United States Treasury.

A bootlegger occasionally used a freight car only as the second step of his journey. Seeking to avoid the sharp eye of customs at the railroad yards, he brought his contraband across the border by highway and then tried to ship it south by train. But he was more vulnerable because he had to be on the spot to make the arrangements. Five hundred cases of ale were discovered on a siding near Plattsburgh, labelled "hay" and hidden behind thirty bales of the feed. Another car got through Plattsburgh but was held at Willsboro and found to contain 200 cases of ale labelled "Empire Oil Barrels." One local shipper tried to send liquor as "apples," but Officer W. F. Scales knew the season was not right for apples and discovered ale instead.

Members of a train crew sometimes tried a little smuggling on the side. Three trainmen went to jail when fifty-six bottles of whiskey were discovered in the caboose. A Negro porter was held when a choice selection of liquor was discovered in the kitchen of a Delaware and Hudson train; he tried to accuse the officers of planting the liquor. Another porter went to federal court when Walter Connelly found twelve bottles of scotch concealed in the refrigerator of a club car. What a railroad employee did in order to serve passengers was apparently his own responsibility and not the railroad's. Pat Goodrow once suspected that an engineer was smuggling liquor concealed in his load of coal. The engineer proving uncooperative, Pat had to shovel the coal aside in what turned out to be a vain search. At the engineer's insistence, Pat had to shovel all the coal back in place. For a long time his friends teased him by asking, "Pat, have you shovelled any coal lately?"

The most notorious case of bootlegging that involved train crews occurred in 1921. Four employees removed 200 cases of liquor concealed in hay from a car on the siding at Bluff Point and hid them in the local station. In order to do so, they had to break the seal on the car and also break into the station, which was closed for the season. The railroad men insisted that they were only doing their duty when they removed contraband from the car. The trouble was that they had not reported their activities. The liquor was probably loaded at Chazy and it was consigned to New Bedford, Massachusetts, where it would have brought $30,000.

Bootlegging on Lake Champlain also presented formidable challenges to both hunter and hunted, and similarly produced ingenious methods of smuggling. The small-scale smuggler shuttled a rowboat back and forth across the border at night. He was hard to detect, and he had any number of landing places in the Rouses Point area. Living quarters on boats and barges also hid small quantities of liquor, most likely for the use of the captain and his family or some of the crew.

Customs officers made their biggest hauls along the shore, where boats reported at customs or stopped for other reasons, including unloading. The seizure of a 45-horsepower boat at Port Henry yielded 150 cases of Black Horse ale. But the biggest capture in the entire North Country, made by Roy Delano at Rouses Point, was 2,000 barrels of bottled ale hidden beneath some lumber on the *E. Daneau*. It was one of a fleet of five barges that had passed through the canal on the Richelieu River, all of them consigned to the Donnor Lumber Company of New York. The other four were legitimately loaded with lumber or hay. The attention of customs officers was first attracted to the *E.*

Daneau by the way it sat in the water. The visible cargo, poor-grade ash lumber, was not heavy enough to make it ride so low. An intensive search revealed a trap door under the cabin cookstove which opened into a space under the lumber big enough to hold all the ale. The quickly-offered explanation was that the shipment had been destined for a Canadian town on the Richelieu and that the barge-master had misunderstood his instructions. Nevertheless, he and the deckhand were held for federal court at Binghamton.

A boat, unlike an automobile, could not be jacked up to make it ride high in the water, making it conspicuous when it was loaded and barely out of water. Furthermore, unusual reconnoitering of the shoreline sometimes aroused the curiosity of the Lake Patrol. Such activity was plentiful south of Rouses Point because many bootleggers, in order to avoid the hazards at the railroad bridge and the narrows where the lake flowed into the Richelieu River, brought liquor by land and loaded it into boats for the run south. One craft, loaded in the Big Chazy River near Champlain, was caught at Fiske's Landing on Isle la Motte. A typical chase was one near Cumberland Head. About to be overtaken, the smugglers jumped into the water and swam for shore, where they were captured. They were allowed to buy dry clothes, however, before being taken to the United States commissioner. Life and limb were not in as much danger as they were on land, and only one man, a customs officer, lost his life on the lake. In a pursuit from the railroad bridge at Rouses Point south to Cumberland Head, Louis Babcock of Waterbury, Vermont, was swept overboard in the wake of the fleeing craft. Another officer leaped into the fugitive boat and forced the pilot to turn back and help search for the body. Almost 500 bottles of assorted liquors were poured over the side, only a little being kept as evidence.

The "submarine," towed behind a fast cruiser, was supposed to sink if, during a pursuit, the smugglers cut it loose. But one such craft was seized after a chase when it unaccountably did not sink and was found carrying 5,000 quarts of ale. Another with 4,000 quarts was captured by the end of a 175-foot hawser when the submarine did not submerge quickly enough. Still another with 4,800 quarts was captured in a boarding operation north of Fort Montgomery by the Royal Mounted Police of Canada, at the suggestion of Captain J. B. Kendrick of the American lake patrol.

Aware that contraband was still getting up the lake, officers occasionally inspected vessels at Whitehall and points south, guessing that the smugglers' vigilance might be relaxed. Such efforts were sometimes rewarded, as when the *Massagna* was being unloaded of 48,000 bottles of ale at Fort Edward. The boat and contents were seized and the captain, engineer, and fireman arrested. One hundred and fifty cases of the unloaded ale were discovered in a nearby barn.

On land pursuit was just as exciting as on the water, and often much more hazardous. Dangerous spots dotted the main highways used by the rumrunners. One was the sharp corner leading onto the bridge at Mooers. Numerous accidents occurred there, on a similar curve at the bridge in Champlain, a sharp turn at Beekmantown Corners, and another at Halsey's

Rouses Point area bootleggers (left to right) Sam Racicot, Harry Hunter, and Tommy Chevalier in 1924. *Courtesy of Bertha Monette.*

Corners at the north edge of Plattsburgh. Miner's Woods on Route 9 north of Chazy was a favorite waiting spot for customs officers, as was hilly Poke-O'-Moonshine south of Keeseville. Officers varied their tactics with the terrain. At Miner's Woods they usually lay in wait beside the road, ready for a chase. Even here the best-laid plans of an officer could go awry. Pat Goodrow once prepared an ambush in a Dodge car, waiting for a bootlegger to go by. Sam Racicot obligingly came along with a load of whiskey. At the crucial moment Pat, forgetting the unusual shifting mechanism of a Dodge, slammed his car into reverse and landed in the ditch, where he remained for the next two hours.

Some of the pursuits were quaint and slow-moving, especially in winter. Three men were once captured when they were seen on snowshoes hauling two toboggans over the border. Inspectors abandoned their car and pursued them on snowshoes for a mile; the toboggan carried 157 bottles of Canadian and foreign liquors concealed under a white canvas. A bobsled was stopped on the Ridge Road south of Champlain and found to contain 246 bottles of assorted liquors in the hollow space between a double floor. Large quantities of liquor came over the fields in winter for the smugglers could avoid the customs stations. Gaston Monette, who engaged in the activity, tells of convoys of five or six teams going through at one time.

One summer Henry Thwaits had an adventure which must have been unexpected to his quarry. Near Silver Lake he intercepted a bootlegger by using a short cut over an abandoned road, but the driver escaped. Just as Thwaits was locking the loaded car another one appeared around the bend. After a short chase the driver abandoned his car and started running across a potato field. Thwaits drove over the bumpy ground and overtook his man, but he had to call for help to get his own car out of the mud. In less than ten minutes he had captured two cars, their contents, and one driver.

Officers developed a variety of devices and strategems that helped them trap many bootleggers. They studded a six-foot sheet of iron with spikes and attached ropes at each end. If a car failed to stop on challenge, two officers stationed down the road pulled the iron in front of the approaching vehicle and invariably made a seizure because the spikes ruined the tires. At other spots, they erected barricades consisting of two or more cars, or a heavy chain across the road. Tommy Chevelier, famous for his robust driving, once approached such a chain. Shifting into second gear, he struck it with such force that he carried it five miles before feeling safe enough to stop and remove it from his car.

Goldy Clark operated a loading station north of Perrys Mills. One night Robert Angell, the agent in charge at Mooers, received a tip from a disaffected bootlegger that liquor was going to be taken from Perrys Mills to Mooers. Fourteen state troopers and federal agents took a stand at a turn in the road where the runners would have to slow down. There they stopped some empty pilot cars, placed them across the road, and subsequently captured thirteen cars that night; all of the drivers jumped and ran amid much shooting on both sides.

Officers sometimes tried to lull bootleggers into thinking they were safe. Thwaits and two other officers lunched one day in Keeseville, aware that they were being watched to see which direction they went. They started for Au Sable Forks but at Clintonville cut across to Reber, on Route 9 south of Keeseville. In a few minutes they stopped a Cadillac loaded with beer. They then halted a truckload of lumber. As they approached it the officers noticed an alcoholic odor. A broken bottle betrayed the smugglers, and 105 cases of champagne were discovered packed under the lumber. The rumrunners used a farmhouse just outside Keeseville as a transfer point, and their pilot had mistakenly called an all-clear signal.

But bootleggers developed schemes of their own

to thwart their pursuers. Two officers were once patrolling the road near Honeymoore's Corners in Chazy when five cars passed them at high speed. They gave chase, but the rear car, driven by Arsene Gload, slowed down to twenty miles an hour and maintained that speed for four miles. He was stopped only when the officers shot his tires, but the other four cars had made good their escape.

Gload was not a unique example of a smuggler in a caravan helping his friends to escape, even if he was himself captured. Early one morning in August 1923, eleven cars approaching Plattsburgh in single file were halted by federal officers. Five of the eleven drivers got away while Lawrence Russets of Schenectady distracted the officers. Russets was taken to the Champlain Valley Hospital with a bullet hole below his left knee, while the other five went to jail. Russets was examined in the hospital next day and held under $1,000 bail. That night he escaped from the hospital. He was neither the first nor the last to do so because no one solved the problem of guarding federal prisoners when they could not be lodged in jail.

Rumrunners learned to force officers off the road, usually during an attempt to pass in order to intercept them. McCrea and Hackmeister both suffered this indignity. Border Patrolman James Hughes once chased a rumrunner's vehicle and its pilot car from Champlain through Chazy to Ingraham. The pilot slowed down to force him off the road. The first attempt knocked the hub cap from the right front wheel. The second did no damage. The third smashed the running board and fender on the right side and forced the inspector into the ditch. He drove back onto the road and continued in pursuit of the two cars but lost them in the streets of Plattsburgh.

Henry Thwaits was closing in on his quarry in a hot pursuit when a high-powered rifle put two bullets through his radiator and one through the body of his car, forcing him to abandon the chase. On another occasion two armed agents signalled an approaching car to stop. The bootleggers speeded up and escaped through a hail of bullets. The agents swerved to avoid a head-on collision, went off the road, and turned over. Near Keeseville a pursuer's car was sent into the ditch, enabling the rumrunner to take a wounded companion to a doctor in Schroon Lake and eventually to the hospital in Ticonderoga. Firing at agents became a common phenomenon in the North Country, and pitched battles usually followed an outbreak of gunfire.

Bootleggers had other strategems for avoiding capture. One man, arrested and wearing handcuffs, was forced by officers to drive his own car into Plattsburgh from the edge of town. He probably deliberately allowed it to get out of control and crash into the Nash business block. The bootlegger did not escape, but he caused difficulties when Nash brought action against the agents. Rumrunners sometimes strewed the path of pursuing agents with glass and nails. William Reil of Bloomingdale threw bottles of whiskey into the road, but his plan misfired when he wrecked his car and was caught. Twenty-one-year-old Elijah "Tango" Belgard threw nails into the road. Going at high speed, he failed to make a corner in Mooers Forks and was killed when his car turned over several times.

The chase became a regular aspect of life in the

North Country during Prohibition. Pursuer and pursued risked their lives and property at high speeds over bad roads amid much gunfire. Both sides seem to have led charmed lives, for fatalities were relatively few and injuries were not commensurate with the number of bullets expended. An officer typically tried to stop a smuggler's car by firing at its vital parts. Tires were the worst, according to bootlegger Gaston Monette: "If you were going at any rate of speed, they shot a tire out from under you, boy, you're liable to pile up somewhere." Or it might be a punctured radiator or gas tank that forced the bootlegger to slow down. Even then, the driver was usually able to escape into the woods, but it is remarkable how far some of them went with flat tires or boiling radiators before finally jumping out and running away. One bootlegger kept up his flight for thirty-three miles with an overheated engine.

Philip Auer tells of a chase that started at the border. A car came across with its lights off, and he started to follow it without his lights. The driver of the lead car apparently suspected someone was behind him, because he began to weave from side to side. Every time he hit one side of the road, off would come a bag of liquor. Then he swerved to the other side, and off would come another bag. Whether to lighten the load or to destroy the evidence Auer could not tell, but he apprehended the bootleggers in Plattsburgh. Then he went back and picked up seven bags, with most of the bottles smashed, that had been thrown off.

Some chases *did* end in accidents and serious injury for the bootlegger. He might, if he was daring enough, jump from his moving car, which would then crash. Through careless driving or the skill of his pursuers he might end up in the ditch, sometimes intact, sometimes badly wrecked. Victor St. Dennis of Plattsburgh was captured at Miner's Woods after his car turned over in the ditch; he had jumped before the crash. Bootleggers ran into telephone poles, stone walls, and once even into the caboose of a freight train at a Plattsburgh crossing. Even more spectacular was a crash at Beekmantown Corners. Pursued at high speed all the way from Mooers, the driver was unable to make the turn, his car rolled over twice and landed on its roof. He escaped, apparently uninjured, into the nearby woods. Since this occurred in 1930, perhaps he did make the eighty mile an hour speed which was reported at the time.

Officers also had their share of untimely accidents. Don Sneeden tried to head off a rumrunner near Halsey's Corners and lost control of his car. He smashed through a number of cement posts and finally rolled over. Blanchard Thompson on a motorcycle pursued a booze car through the business district of Plattsburgh. The chase ended when Thompson ran into a telephone pole.

One of the most desperate confrontations occurred on the "Rum Trail" south of Elizabethtown in 1924. Henry Thwaits and two assistants captured a caravan of four cars near North Hudson. Then they saw a Cadillac sedan approaching. Its driver tried to turn around but was stopped with a bullet in the gas tank. The driver and a female companion escaped. Next, a truck came roaring down the road. It turned and fled, with the law in pursuit. The driver escaped, but the truck was captured and brought back to make a sixth prize. Meanwhile, a crowd had gathered and begun to snatch bottles from the seized cars. Without warning, a member of the crowd jumped into the truck and sped away, vainly pursued by Thwaits. Then the crowd advanced upon the outnumbered officers, covering them with revolvers. They recaptured two of the cars and roared away. The crowning humiliation to the officers, after the dust of battle had settled, was to discover that Thwait's tires had been slashed to ribbons.

Some of the pursuits covered more than half the length of the county. One of the longest was a chase by Officers Coveney and Smith from Ingraham through Plattsburgh to Au Sable Forks. When finally overtaken, two men jumped and fled, leaving the female companion to be apprehended. One of the men was subsequently captured on foot after a chase of a mile.

At five o'clock one morning in 1922, Philip Lafountaine and his 18-year-old son refused to stop their Peerless sedan for Hamilton McCrea at Halsey's Corners. A particularly wild chase ensued through Plattsburgh. With a chauffeur at the wheel, McCrea from the running board of his car exchanged shot for shot with the Lafountaines, hitting their car at least twenty times. Twice McCrea's car passed the Peerless as it sped through the main section of Plattsburgh, but Lafountaine only laughed when ordered to halt. Many citizens were rudely awakened by the cars roaring past at fifty miles an hour and by the fusillade of bullets. A tire on the Peerless was hit as it moved onto the Peru road, but not for several miles did the car be-gin to lose speed. McCrea was able to get out in front and block the road, and there the running battle ended as suddenly as it began.

The chase is best celebrated in a ballad in praise of a notorious Packard car, whose owner lived in Gabriels, New York.

BERT LA FONTAINE'S PACKARD

'Twas on a Sunday morning I headed for
    the north—
The road I often travelled while riding back
    and forth;
I crossed the old St. Lawrence, going straight
    to Montreal
With Bert La Fontaine's Packard for a load
    of alcohol.

Well, I loaded her with liquor, and I stocked
    her with wine and ale;
To get across the border I knew I must not
    fail;
But they signalled me with flashlights and
    ordered me to halt,
But I tore right by the customs house with
    La Fontaine's alcohol.

The troopers and immigrationers, to them I
    paid no heed,
I was rolling eighty and putting on the speed;
I was going straight through Merrill and
    headed for Malone,
When word got ahead of me—'twas by a
    telephone.

108

I saw the troopers' barrier and a car across
    the road,
I quickly left the wheel, the Packard, and the
    load;
I'm waiting for my trial, which is to come
    this fall,
It's now I'm out on bail and I know I lost
    it all.

Aside from reckless pursuits through the city, Plattsburgh had many other problems during the Prohibition era. It was the most populated center in northeastern New York, and several of the smugglers' trails converged upon it. It consequently became an important transfer point as well as the location of many "joints" designed to assuage the thirst of the local citizenry. Multiple raids became a regular event in the city for many years. The streets that won most consistent fame were Bridge, Peru, Charlotte, Elizabeth, and U.S. Avenue, but no part of the city was immune.

Many of the raids were conducted by the city police, sometimes accompanied by military police or federal officers. But so many of the raids failed to find liquor that it was suspected someone in the police department was leaking information. Federal agents, therefore, conducted surprise raids on their own. The culmination of federal activity came in February 1925, when fifty-five agents simultaneously raided spots along the "Rum Trail" from Albany to Plattsburgh. They arrested thirty-six people and seized liquor worth $60,000.

Most of the raids, however, were less spectacular. Officers had to be on the lookout for three types of enterprises: transfer stations, usually rented garages; the sale of illegal beverages by the drink; and the manufacture of home brew. More than one of these activities might be carried on at the same address. Until 1929 all raids had to be conducted under the authority of a search warrant, and illegal operators soon became expert in challenging the legal limitations of a particular warrant. After 1929 federal officers were authorized to search private property merely on suspicion that it contained contraband.

Officials received tips about the "hot spots" from a variety of sources. A disgruntled neighbor might complain about the disorderly house next door (a raid might uncover liquor as well as slot machines and other illegal devices), or a captured bootlegger might confess and reveal his Plattsburgh destination. A telephone call from the parents of missing youngsters sometimes produced startling results: two girls, ages fourteen and sixteen, were once traced to a "joint" on Boynton Avenue, Plattsburgh, where they were found intoxicated. Raids sometimes followed the complaint of a person who asserted that he had been beaten or robbed at a specified address.

During 1922 numerous raids were based on the tips of one "Henry Ellsworth," who was never publicly identified but who was thought to be connected with the Twenty-sixth Infantry at the Plattsburgh Barracks. The military was interested in drying up the environs of the barracks, and the provost marshal and military police collaborated frequently in raids conducted by city police. First-hand information about the activities of a suspected "soft-drink parlor" was often gathered by federal officers in plain clothes who bought alcoholic drinks on the premises before they quietly left to get a warrant.

To be effective raids had to be conducted suddenly, and they sometimes involved smashing through doors. Officers were not so much interested in the patrons as they were the operators of the place. They learned to act quickly to prevent the escape of owner or bartender and the destruction of the evidence. Time allowing, operators tried to hide the liquor or pour it down the drain, and many a tussle took place between bartender and officer for custody of an incriminating bottle. If the bartender was caught with the evidence, the owner might plead that he was not responsible for the activities of his employees, and if he was acquitted in court he was free to continue business at the old stand. The history of Plattsburgh raids is one of repeated visits to the same address by enforcement agents, until the ultimate weapon of padlocking was finally employed.

Raids on Peru Street and elsewhere uncovered garages containing truckloads of liquor awaiting reshipment. The Sunrise Hotel west of the city was such a place, but a raid was aborted there by a defective search warrant. A raid on the Auto Inn on the Lake Shore Road revealed a veritable oasis of assorted liquors, but not before the bartender and the chef tried to flee with some of the evidence. Even some of the barber shops of the city were discovered to be dispensing drinks to their customers.

Confrontation between law and outlaw can be highlighted by the case histories of two notorious characters, both of whom proved remarkably durable in spite of repeated setbacks. Dick Warner of Saratoga Springs was already on the government's wanted list for bootlegging by the spring of 1920. He and an equally slippery smuggler, Tommy O'Connor of Montreal, were apprehended in Keeseville in March, although both used fictitious names. Despite a new mustache, O'Connor was immediately recognized; to identify the other an acquaintance of Warner in New York City was sent for. Warner was positively identified, closely held in $25,000 bail, and sentenced to two years in the Atlanta penitentiary after pleading guilty to six counts of smuggling liquor. O'Connor also went to jail, for four months.

Less than two years later, free and back in business, Warner, his female companion Dorothy Swartout of Saratoga Springs, and O'Connor were stopped at the border but allowed to proceed when no liquor was discovered in their car. Four hours later the men, minus Dorothy, were caught with liquor in Chazy. They were taken to Rouses Point and locked in the detention room of the customs house. At this point Dorothy prematurely attracted attention by coming to inquire for her husband, "John Fox, Jr." When the officers went to get him they discovered that an iron bar had been torn off the window and that both men had disappeared. Special agents went into Canada, and spotting the fugitives, they obtained Canadian help and besieged the farmhouse where they were thought to be hiding. Captured in the cellar, the smugglers were finally turned over to the American agents despite their vociferous claims of Canadian citizenship. They were jailed in Plattsburgh under $5,000 bail each but were hastily transferred to the Onondaga County jail when it was discovered that two of the bars of their cell window were sawed in half. No saws were ever found, nor had the pair had any visitors. In federal court the two received surprisingly light sentences considering their records, Warner drawing eleven months and O'Connor four.

Thirteen months later Warner and Dorothy were caught north of Beekmantown. No liquor was found in their car, but drivers of the two cars behind them escaped, leaving loads for which he was allegedly the pilot. In federal court, in an action described as "bootlegger's gallantry," Warner pleaded guilty to various charges in order to "take the girl's medicine" as well as his own. He got $10,000 and two years on a conspiracy charge, $2,000 and one year for possession, $2,000 for transporting liquor, and $1 for importing liquor without a license. Warner was said to have accepted it all with a smile and waved to his companions as he was taken to his cell. And so he vanished from the North Country scene.

Another determined rumrunner was Charles "Muskrat" Robare of Keeseville, who smuggled by car and boat, and for good measure operated his own still. He gained his nickname by reputedly swimming his way to freedom during a hot pursuit, and thereafter he wore a muskrat hat. One of his earliest brushes with the law occurred at Wood's Falls when Henry Thwaits tried to stop him. He turned and started for Canada, Thwaits in pursuit. The officer put a bullet in his tire, but Robare drove on a flat tire until he got over the border, several miles away, and then jumped and ran.

A raid on Whitney's Island, off Port Kent, uncovered some beer allegedly owned by Robare, but the case was muddied by the fact that a boat that was confiscated was sold without advertising it. Robare was not convicted. He was involved in the big smuggling ring that eventually sent officers and civilians, but not Robare, to jail. He was, however, convicted of operating a still near Keeseville. On the day of the raid, four men tried to escape across the fields but were caught. Robare hid in the attic and came down only when he heard that his father was about to be arrested. On the basis of his own admission of ownership, he was sent to the Atlanta Penitentiary for a year and a day.

Freed from Atlanta on parole and presumably on good behavior, Robare was arrested in Canada for breaking the liquor laws there. He was fined and sentenced to three months in a Canadian jail, after which he was turned over to American authorities. At his hearing in federal court the deputy marshal testified that he had sold at least ten of Robare's cars, some of them quite new. Charged with violating his parole from Atlanta, he was sent to Leavenworth to finish his term.

After the Prohibition era Robare spent time in prison for car robbery. After that he was charged with murdering Yale Morris with an axe and burying the body on the spot. Following a four-day trial, he hanged himself in his cell. And so passed another notorious character from the North Country.

Confusion in the Countryside

I believe that ninety percent of the people in the county were opposed to prohibition. Not one farmer in twenty-five would not shield, help, or hide a rum-runner. The usual compensation for their help was a bottle of liquor, more highly prized than money.

Henry Thwaits of Au Sable Forks

As a youngster of fourteen or fifteen I can well remember the cars chasing through the town and going on down to what we called the horse bridge, which had a rather sharp turn, and shots being fired and tires squealing as they made the curve and upon occasion somebody being wrecked and the local doctors being dragged out to take care of the people who had been hit.

Howard S. Curtis, formerly of Mooers

T HIRSTY PEOPLE during Prohibition had their choice of "soft-drink parlors," "blind pigs," speakeasies, and "dives" in Plattsburgh, Rouses Point, Au Sable Forks, and other centers of population, and these were busy places indeed. The more sophisticated patrons, however, disliked the furtiveness of such operations, the rot-gut that was often served, and the risk of being caught in a raid. To satisfy their needs Canadian entrepreneurs opened night clubs at convenient spots along their border with New York. One of the best known was the Meridian Hotel, just north of Cham-

115

plain. It served good food and reasonably-priced drinks, and its band and dance floor provided facilities for a lively evening. The Meridian and others like it thrived during the Depression years. Americans by the hundreds went there, especially on Saturdays and holidays; on New Year's Eve of 1932, reservations totalled 1,200. Some couples in Plattsburgh still remember their first trip in the early spring, when they followed a narrow road between snowdrifts higher than their cars, with turnouts for maintaining two-way traffic. The operators of the village snowplow at Champlain once tried to serve the patrons of the Meridian, as Roy Delano delightedly recalls, even though it was located across the border. After a fresh fall of snow the plow fell into the cesspool of the hotel. Suppressing the news proved impossible, and as word spread, so did the hilarity.

The clientele with their hundreds of cars all had to funnel through the village of Champlain and north on Oak Street to the border. Their return late at night disturbed the sleep of the residents, especially on Saturdays when the screeching of brakes marked the approach to the bridge over the river. Smash-ups occurred with such regularity that, as Woody McLellan comments, "It got so we would wait up for it because every Saturday night there would be an accident."

The Meridian was only one of the border hotels. Others included the Lacolle Inn, the Tourist Garden Hotel, and the Hotel Bouillon. They took half-page advertisements in the Plattsburgh papers, frequently printing directions about the best routes for getting there. Catering to those who wanted a stouter evening

The Meridian Hotel, one of the most popular Canadian border spots, attracted large crowds from the United States,
especially on the weekends. This hotel was the scene of the
embarrassing fall of the Champlain snowplow into a septic
tank.

were such spots as the Broken Knuckle, north of
Rouses Point, and the Bucket of Blood, across the
road from the Meridian. The Broken Knuckle had a
slot machine which took in a great deal of money. Jack
Ross remembers that an American went there one
night and set the rear of the building afire. Then he
ran inside to spread the alarm and when everyone
dashed to deal with the fire he made off with the slot

Captioned "Land of the Free," this photo, taken in Canada between Rouses Point, N.Y., and Lacolle, Quebec, shows typical Canadian advertising during Prohibition.

machine. Just north of Rouses Point he opened it with an axe and got away with all its contents.

For several years this evening traffic in and out of Canada was treated casually by customs officers on both sides of the border, except where smuggling was suspected. But in 1927 the United States attempted to seal the border by requiring Americans to register at the American customs house, where they were given a permit and told to report to Canadian customs. This meant that although the American customs was closed

118

by eleven o'clock, returning Americans were supposed to find an officer, even if it meant getting him out of bed. The alternative, for innocent merrymakers, was to be considered still in Canada or to be regarded as a rumrunner who had deliberately avoided checking into the country.

The dollar flow into Canada from the activities of bootleggers and night-lifers was partially compensated for by the flow of money from downstate New York and New England to the rural areas along the northern border. Money changed hands rapidly as bootleggers used their gains for new cars, furs, clothes, and even houses. The brittle prosperity of the 1920s existed in the North Country, buttressed to some extent by rumrunning profits. A *New York Times* study in 1932 concluded that Prohibition had made rural Vermont better off, and that repeal might create unemployment and hard times for the hotels that served tourists on their way to Canada.

In many small ways some citizens of the North Country benefited from Prohibition without being involved in smuggling. From time to time federal authorities directed the gift of some of the best brands of impounded whiskey to hospitals for medicinal purposes. Sometimes political office could be gained even by a man who was known to dislike Prohibition. For example, Postmaster George Rivers of Rouses Point was respected by the young bootleggers of the town, and he reciprocated their regard. A group of them organized a campaign and got him overwhelmingly elected mayor. Unfortunately, he was forced to refuse the office because he did not meet the property qualifications.

119

Government auctions of seized property such as hay, lumber, sleighs, horses, and cars were a boon to citizens in the neighborhood. Old cars sold for as little as $35. The purchase of such a car sometimes included unexpected surprises. The wife of one customs officer bought a car which she used for about two years. When the seat cushion did not seem to fit properly, it was unfastened and found to conceal half a dozen bottles of liquor which had not been discovered when the car was originally seized. Charles Curtis of Mooers bought an auctioned vehicle to use on his rural mail routes; it looked so much like a bootlegger's car that he was stopped by new officers in the area and made to explain why he was using the back roads so often. Perhaps he forgot that it would also have to double as the family car, and his son remembers the uncomfortable Sunday outings when the family rode hard and high on reinforced springs.

Gifts of whiskey were often a mark of esteem for the family doctor, lawyer, neighbor, or anyone else who had done the bootlegger a service. Some of the people on Curtis's mail route left him Christmas bottles in their mailboxes. Being a teetotaler, he stored them at home and when they were needed he used their contents as antifreeze in the radiator of his car. Hugh McLellan of Champlain was another recipient. He once offered his barn for storage of baled hay impounded from a freight car. Each bale contained a case of liquor which he later learned was the property of his own employee. A few days later he found a case of champagne on his doorstep, apparently salvaged from the seizure. McLellan put it in a small safe and one night frightened off robbers who had dragged it halfway to the front door. The champagne was given to friends and enjoyed at home—all except the last bottle, which was opened on his eightieth birthday in 1954 and was too flat to be tasty!

But Prohibition did not hand out favors impartially. Many residents of Clinton County found the 1920s not a game but a nightmare. Time has mellowed their outlook so that now they can look back with amusement and not a little fondness. But at the time, parents raised sons who defied the dangers of bootlegging and sometimes landed in the penitentiary. Daughters worried their elders with their "fast" boyfriends and rounds of the speakeasies. Neighbors were sometimes alienated when they differed sharply over the Prohibition law. Many came to suspect all law enforcement agencies because of the rumors about official corruption and favoritism. Reports of violence along the border titillated the adventurous while it outraged the law-abiding.

There were many pitfalls for the innocent but unwary. Anyone in the path of a pursuit was in some danger. It might be no worse than a farmer's hogs getting drunk when a fleeing bootlegger flung his wares into the pig pen, or perhaps nothing more than a load of beer which officers smashed in Elmer Caron's cow path in Churubusco; he had to cover the broken glass before his cows could use the path again.

Lavinia Bullis, who lived with her husband near the border in Champlain, tells of being in her yard when shots were fired in the road and of being so frightened one time that she crawled in the cellar window of her home. She and her husband, while working outside one day, saw a man conceal his liquor in their culvert. He then reported to customs in Rouses Point, came back to look for his loot, and was surprised to find it still there. He tried to give the Bullises some of the liquor and when they refused, he insisted that they take five dollars instead.

More serious were the damages to civilian lives and property. A rum car ran onto a lawn in Chazy before the bootlegger could bring it under control. Trees and shrubs were regular casualties. Buildings were sometimes hit, especially in Plattsburgh. Mrs. Daniel Hanks' car was badly damaged near the high school in Plattsburgh when it was hit by a bootlegger's car; the driver, Nolan ("One-arm") Chapman, jumped from his own car while it was still moving. Innocent drivers suffered bad accidents when a furious pursuit swirled around them. At least one horse and driver, Joseph Barcomb of Chazy, were killed when they were struck by a racing rumrunner.

Indeed, the use of some of the roads by law-abiding citizens was so risky at night that many of them stayed at home. Unnumbered collisions were narrowly avoided when bootleggers drove at high speeds without lights. The road through Miner's Woods was dreaded by travelers because it was so often the scene of patrolmen's efforts to catch smugglers. Travelers tried to avoid completely any night driving over Poke-O'-Moonshine because it was such a funnel for reckless rumrunning. Innocent citizens were held up occasionally by hijackers looking for liquor. In one such instance, when the citizens tried to defend themselves two of them went to the hospital with bullet wounds.

Mrs. Russell Conger sought the district attorney when her car was shot through the rear window by a customs officer at the Rouses Point customs house, and the bullet missed her by inches; a "mistake" was admitted at the border. Most of the complaints came from residents of Plattsburgh whose lives were endangered on the streets of the city or who were awakened in the middle of the night by gunfire that sometimes broke their windows.

Prohibition raised havoc with discipline and attendance at public schools along the border. Howard Curtis recalls the holiday atmosphere that surrounded destruction of liquor at the town dump, when he and his friends played hookie from school to watch the proceedings. Liquor was thrown down a deep and rocky ravine in the expectation, not always realized, that every bottle would break. A patrolman sometimes added to the excitement by shooting into the bags. After the officers left, the youngsters climbed down into the rubble and occasionally found an unbroken bottle, which they sold to a villager for a sum "that made them feel well rewarded for their efforts."

As if this were not enough for the Mooers' principal, the boys also took off on the days of "booze sales," the auctioning of seized cars. Despite a warning, three boys still cut classes to go to a sale, and they were expelled. Unfortunately for the principal, the fathers of the three were the chairman of the school board, the supervisor of the town, and an influential merchant. Needless to say, the boys were all back in school next day. Meanwhile, drinking at school games and dances became a new daring adventure. Curtis tells of coughing over his first drink of whiskey, Golden Wedding, when it was passed around the boys' locker room, after which he had to go back to history class.

Prohibition news filled the columns of the newspapers of northern New York, and it sometimes placed the editors in a quandary. The *Plattsburgh Republican* illustrates this difficulty. Owned and managed locally, its policy at first was a cautious support of Prohibition, out of deference to its many dry subscribers. From the beginning its managers disliked the law, but although they conceded in 1921 that "a certain number of average good citizens don't like prohibition," they thought the real question was: "Do we believe in law?" Its continued flaunting would mean "good night to this nation as the home of the free," because anarchy would surely follow. In 1922 it praised a Canadian proposal to collect income taxes from its own rumunners as worthy of duplication in the United States. It also deplored the canard being spread about North Country lawlessness which, if not refuted, would frighten vacationers away from the Adirondacks.

In 1923 the paper advocated a state referendum to ascertain the "will of the people" on Prohibition. A year later, in an editorial entitled "Prohibition a Failure," for the first time it proposed the modification of the Volstead Act to make it enforceable. Warming to this theme, the editor declared: "Because the Volstead Act is unenforceable it is an influence toward anarchy. It is the duty of the Governor to administer it as well as he can, the duty of those who see it as an inherently vicious statute to agitate for its revision."

The paper developed its policy of opposition during the rest of the era, becoming sharper in its denunciations with the passing years. In 1926 it believed that "the prohibition house of cards is crumbling." It desired a national referendum in the presidential election year of 1928. In the following year it advocated reform in the name of "life, liberty and the pursuit of happiness," and two months later it charged that "the unbelievable has happened and in our times organized minorities are actively engaged in persecuting majorities." Referring in 1930 to the "fanaticism of prohibition," it declared that "the tragic experiment produces a kind of circular insanity in which one ancient liberty after another is ruthlessly abandoned." It backed the Democratic repeal platform in 1932 and rejoiced over the end of Prohibition.

The editor reserved some of his harshest criticism for the shootings that occurred during pursuits, and he especially blamed customs officers, forgetting that many of the bootleggers were armed as well. When a bullet passed a few inches from the bed in which the Duquettes were sleeping on Bailey Avenue, public officials joined the hue and cry. Mayor William E. Cross wrote a moderate letter of protest to Robert D. Angell, head of the Malone customs office: "An officer with the best intentions in enforcing the law but with a poor or uncertain aim may cause injury to innocent persons. The existence of conditions where honest and law-abiding citizens are afraid to travel our roads between sunset and sunrise is, I need hardly say, something which neither you nor I wish to have continued. We have been proud to call this section a playground but really did not think when we said it that it would come to mean gunplay." Declaring that "the enforcement of law is the object of both of us," he asked that

125

the use of guns be minimized so that "at the same time that we are trying to drive the bootlegger from our roads, let us not try to drive the tourists and pleasure seekers away also."

The situation was eased temporarily by directives from Malone. But by 1926 the *Republican* was inveighing against customs officers who allegedly had put eleven bullets into the car of an innocent citizen in Chazy. Congressman Bertrand H. Snell of Malone, who raised the issue of border shootings in Washington, received assurances that agents would be ordered not to use firearms unless they were attacked or faced with extreme provocation and not to use them at all in the towns. Despite such directives, shootings eventually were resumed, as bullets in tires or gas tanks were the officers' main hope of stopping a rumrunner, and in any case patrolmen could with justification consider themselves "under attack" from the bullets of the bootleggers.

Shootings in 1929 led to protests by both District Attorney B. Loyal O'Connell and Mayor John H. McGaulley, who declared that good citizens wanted the law to be enforced but deplored the shootings in the streets of Plattsburgh. John C. Tulloch, collector of customs in Ogdensburg, promised that such incidents would not happen again because officers would be prohibited from using arms within city limits. Nevertheless, an exceptionally wild chase through the main part of Plattsburgh occurred in 1930, with speeds of seventy-five miles an hour and bullets flying in disregard of the many people on the streets. The problem was never solved while Prohibition lasted, and it probably helped many people to conclude that the law itself was responsible.

Prohibitionists shared with other Americans a profound faith in the power of new laws to solve problems. They also reflected the nation's puritanical tradition when they decided that the consumption of alcohol was morally and socially wrong. For them a great social evil was on the verge of eradication with the mere passage of the Volstead Act. When the act proved difficult to enforce, they attributed this to human greed, which they were confident would soon be overcome. In 1924 Wayne B. Wheeler of the Anti-Saloon League announced that drinking was down by ninety percent; he reached this conclusion with statistics showing a drastic decline in the amount of money spent for alcoholic beverages. In 1922 a poll of college presidents showed that 136 favored Prohibition, while only 22 were noncommittal or opposed. In 1926 college administrators thought that student drinking had decreased. Irving Fisher, the Yale economist, asserted that six billion dollars was being saved by the nation for the release of its human energies and skills. Secretary of Commerce Hoover had already made a similar declaration.

The Women's Christian Temperance Union and the Anti-Saloon League could rightly claim, along with several Protestant church denominations, to be the leading instigators of national Prohibition. After 1920 both groups remained active for a few years, seemed to relax during the middle 1920s, and then, as attacks on the law became more alarming, sprang to a vigorous defense. They were joined in 1922 by the

Women's National Committee for Law Enforcement which, at the end of ten years, claimed to represent twelve million women. All of them were organized nationally and statewide, and the WCTU also had organizations in northern New York which met regularly.

In 1920 well-known speakers from the Anti-Saloon League appeared in the pulpits of forty local churches to urge the enactment of a state enforcement law paralleling the Volstead Act. The most cooperative denominations were the Methodist, Baptist and Presbyterian, and most of the visiting speakers spoke from their pulpits. Moreover, many of the meetings of the WCTU were held in those churches. Meetings were conducted along the lines of a Protestant church service and included singing, prayer, Bible reading, and an address. Mrs. D. Leigh Colvin, the state president, sometimes presided. Her remarks were usually sharp, and she once likened the current situation to the Whiskey Rebellion of 1794, a lawless revolt that had to be put down by force. At one meeting a local member presented a bottle of milk, a loaf of bread, and a toy as the things children would lose with repeal, then "the afternoon closed pleasantly with a social hour and refreshments."

The "white-ribboners," as the members of the WCTU were known, gave five local prizes in 1922 ranging from $1–5 for the best eighth-grade essays on Prohibition. The president of the State Anti-Saloon League, Fred A. Victor, once spoke in the Plattsburgh Methodist Church. He recounted the nation's blessings under Prohibition: more money in the banks; more young people in high school, since they did not have to help support the family; a great increase in life insurance; and fewer women sentenced for drunkenness. Pussyfoot Johnson spoke from the same rostrum. A noted dry advocate, his tour was sponsored by the World League Against Alcoholism. He predicted after a trip to India that the world would be dry in ten years if the American efforts at Prohibition continued to succeed. Mrs. Henry Peabody, chairman of the Women's National Committee for Law Enforcement, also appeared in the Methodist Church, as did Vida Mulholland, chairman of the state committee. Peabody enumerated three previous rebellions against the Constitution, with a fourth now going on. All of these groups wanted to prevent any tampering with their momentous reform, and they used their time-honored tactics of exhortation and statistics, mingling their ideas with religious sentiment in a setting of luncheons and social hours to achieve this end.

But the decade of the 1920s confirmed the worst fears of the opponents of Prohibition and converted many former proponents. President Ernest M. Hopkins of Dartmouth College said in 1930 that he had hoped for a great deal of good but instead saw more liquor being drunk and a powerful underworld created. Attorney General John C. Sargent placed the blame squarely upon the respectable citizen who bribed another to violate the Volstead Act: "Every person who sells liquor does it solely and only because someone will pay a price high enough to make a profit sufficient to offset the chance of detection, conviction and punishment."

Many North Country residents fell within the purview of Sargent's denunciation. One former customs officer now calls it a "bum law"; another says, with some exaggeration, that 90 percent of the population was opposed to it. Almost everyone who lived during the period is certain that it led to increased drinking. Two prominent Plattsburgh attorneys assert that members of families who never drank before began to view drinking, hip flasks, and the speakeasy as new and exciting aspects of life. One of these, Jeremiah Davern, declares that the Prohibition law made mob rule possible and that it put money and power into the hands of the wrong people. It bred hostility toward all law enforcement officers which was fanned into flame with every shooting incident. It tended to make folk-heroes out of the rumrunners and relegated officers of the law to the role of "bad guys."

Howard Curtis, recalling his boyhood in Mooers, says that the law was not very highly regarded by respectable people because the leaders of the town had liquor delivered to their homes either by bootleggers or, occasionally, by border patrolmen. Young people consequently had difficulty in taking the law very seriously. A few citizens of Plattsburgh had the foresight to obtain a legal permit for liquor they owned prior to July 1, 1919, but most of them were willing to deal with bootleggers indefinitely. Some idea of the appetite that developed can be seen in the aftermath of an auto accident involving a loaded car in the village of Champlain. Before the customs officers could arrive, says Woody McLellan, the car had been emptied of its beer, and the mayor of the village, among others, was caught and fined for trying to get away with a sack. On Margaret Street, in the heart of Plattsburgh's shopping district, customs officers seized an eighty-bag carload of liquor but left it unguarded for a few minutes. A large crowd gathered and made off with much of the load in a short time.

Destruction of captured liquor also brought out the crowds. Before taking it to the dump in Plattsburgh (at the mouth of the Saranac River), sacks of liquor were carried from the federal building to waiting trucks. The employee who stood at the rear of the truck managed to remove a bottle from each sack and pass it into the crowd of onlookers. There it went from hand to hand in an effective, if unplanned, redistribution of the goods. Sheriff Coffey superintended the destruction of liquor in January 1923, before a large crowd which, but for his vigilance, would have clambered over the broken bottles before all the contents had drained out. The town dump was the usual site for such activities. Invariably, large crowds gathered to gawk and grab. As Gaston Monette tells it, "Most of the time there wasn't enough law there to unload it and break it so civilians would go in and help and while they were such a crowd there that when they'd go by with a bag they'd dump just about half of the bag in the crowd and that was it!"

That Prohibition was not achieving its objective in the North Country can be indicated statistically. Convictions for intoxication increased in Clinton County from 56 in 1921, to 92 in 1922. Convictions for violation of the liquor tax law jumped from 218 in 1920, to 681 in 1921, and 1,646 in 1922. Part of this spectacular increase can be attributed to stricter enforcement under the state's Mullan-Gage law. The Metropolitan Life Insurance Company released statistics showing a startling increase in the national death rate from alcohol: in 1920 the deaths from alcoholism, including wood and poison alcohols, was 1.2 per 100,000 deaths; in 1926 it was 6.3.

Dr. Harrison S. Martland, chief medical examiner for rural Essex County, attributed ninety deaths to alcohol during 1927. Eight were from acute alcoholism, eight from poisoning in which alcohol was a contributing factor, thirty from vehicular accidents which featured intoxicants, and forty-four from falls while people were drunk. The doctor said in his report: "People who drank before prohibition are drinking now, providing they are still alive. Many people who never drank before prohibition now drink, and almost exclusively hard liquor. Instead of licensed saloons open to inspection we have the bootlegging speakeasies, which far outnumber the original unlicensed saloons, and are the decubital sores of our community. Among the younger generation rarely is a party a success unless the high school boy carries his hip flask. Practically all hard liquors are poisonous. It is practically impossible at the present time to purchase whiskey which has not been cut or monkeyed with, and even medical liquors are under suspicion."

The cutting or "monkeying" did not necessarily make whiskey poisonous, although dubious ingredients were often added for coloring and other adulterating purposes. The real threat was industrial alcohol which the government denatured to discourage its human consumption. Government chemists were constantly searching for formulas which would render alcohol impossible to purify. Nevertheless, the product found its way into the rum trade, and deaths and blindness mounted. Plattsburgh seems not to have been afflicted until 1929, when several deaths occurred that were attributed to liquor containing poisoned alcohol. The police department stepped up its raids and appealed to the public for cooperation in getting rid of the poisoned supplies. As usual the police had to carry on the task unaided.

One result of the enforcement of the Prohibition laws was the overcrowded condition of jails both locally and nationwide. Prohibition was credited for the influx at the Leavenworth and Atlanta penitentiaries. The county jail in Plattsburgh was frequently full, with the smugglers of aliens and liquor forming the largest contingent of prisoners. Lack of space sometimes caused the transfer of federal prisoners to the Essex County jail until they were due in court. Clinton County eventually made an arrangement for convicted offenders to serve their sentences in the Onondaga County jail. To local authorities this seemed preferable to the construction of additional facilities.

Civilians by the hundreds became entangled, willingly or otherwise, with the consequences of the Prohibition law. Few were unaffected by its ramifications, but fewer still stepped forward to help enforce it. Instead, they helped the bootlegger, either out of sympathy or for their own profit. Some relayed telephone messages, others flagged down smugglers to warn of danger ahead, and many rented barns and garages as temporary stopping places for loads on the way south. If caught they were not severely dealt with and occasionally, as with a garage on the Tom Miller Road, escaped penalties by declaring that they had rented it to Vermonters and knew nothing about its use. The regular rental of buildings was paid in cash, but more occasional assistance was rewarded by a bottle of liquor, which was often more highly prized than money.

Elmer Caron relates how the subtle forms of help worked. One winter fourteen state troopers out of Malone got stuck in the snow and hired Elmer's father to take them by sleigh to the train at Churubusco. As another sleigh approached, the troopers told Caron to stop, but he managed not to hear them. On more emphatic orders he did stop for the next sleigh, and it was driven by a neighbor who was innocent, but Caron knew that the first sleigh contained another neighbor who was carrying liquor.

Other civilians who tried to keep their distance from the traffic sometimes became involved anyway, especially if they lived along any of the smugglers' routes. Ralph Sanger on Rand Hill recalls that his father refused repeated offers for the rental of his barns, yet bootleggers who had come to grief on Rand Hill regularly arrived at the Sanger door for food or help with their cars. One such experience is indelibly fixed in Ralph's mind because it occurred on his wedding day in 1924. Henry Thwaits had captured a booze car nearby, although its two passengers escaped into the woods. Thwaits was refused permission to break liquor bottles on the Sanger property, and after getting help from Plattsburgh, he went on his way. The two bootleggers then persuaded Ralph to drive them to Peru. For this he was unwilling to accept pay, but they left five dollars on the seat of the car, which Ralph used to pay the minister for marrying him that afternoon. Unfortunately, he forgot what the Peru trip had done to his gas tank, and he ran out of gasoline on the way to his own wedding.

News-gathering companies tried to be on hand to film the more spectacular liquor-seizing activities. Pathé once arrived in Champlain to film a simulated capture at the customs house, but just as the cameras were in place word arrived that a caravan of bootleggers was going south on the Ridge Road. Patrolmen raced to their cars and started in pursuit, with the Pathé man following and hoping to film an actual capture, but the chase in this case proved unsuccessful.

A Keith magician who was performing in Plattsburgh went up to the Meridian for some drinks one evening. On his return he stopped at customs where his car was searched, without result, by Officer Walter Shank. The driver admitted he was too drunk to drive, and he came into the station to wait until he had sobered up. While there he entertained Shank and young Woody McLellan for several hours with a fine array of tricks. He finally offered to make anything appear on request. Uppermost in everyone's mind at the time was liquor, and he was commanded to produce a bottle of whiskey. At first he demurred, knowing that it would be taken away from him. Shank searched him thoroughly and then told him: "You're clean; now if you can make a bottle of whiskey appear, you can keep it." The magician held up a blanket, incanted some mumbo jumbo, and reappeared with a bottle of whiskey in his hand. It was a regular quart bottle and although he must have had it concealed all the time, Shank kept his word, and the magician departed with his prize.

Bartenders who were put out of business by Prohibition found employment in illegal places or turned to the legal retailing of hard cider, which could be found in the apple-growing countryside. Darwin Keysor remembers that hard cider was a profitable stock-in-trade at the Union Hotel, where he worked as a boy. It was consumed in great quantities and Keysor recalls being ordered to dilute it "until the water content was so great it was actually sobering the two men up." Other places discovered, what farmers had long known, that freezing cider produced a concentrate of almost pure alcohol. Indeed, farmers soon awoke to the fact that they possessed a number of new advantages under Prohibition, in addition to their apples. Their abundant harvests of corn began to find their way into mash for the distilling industry, and corn whiskey became the primary product of New York distilleries. The increased demand for hops for the beer-brewing industry gave some farmers an additional cash crop. Even in 1919 an acre of hops brought a return of about $486 an acre to only $21 for corn. Franklin County witnessed a large increase in the cultivation of hops during the Prohibition years.

Denied normal access to alcoholic beverages at reasonable prices, the North Country greatly expanded its production of moonshine whiskey and homebrew beer. A good deal of the activity was concentrated in Plattsburgh, but distilling and brewing were carried on in nearly every town in the county. Crude distilling apparatus could be bought or made and required relatively little space to conceal when not in use. Stills were operated in barns, sheds, and basements. Mrs. Howard Coon used the kitchen fire of her home in Plattsburgh. In Perrys Mills, the Thompson place was rented to new tenants. This sedate old farmhouse began to vibrate with activity, and from it emanated "hen whiskey", locally named because it was distilled in the former hen house. The contemporary quip about "chicken whiskey" was: two drinks, and you don't care where you lay.

Aside from equipment the only other necessity was the mash. If for distilling, the mash was usually made of corn, and the product was corn whiskey. If for beer, the mash consisted of other grains. In 1932 a modern brewery was discovered on Bridge Street in Plattsburgh which made good beer by a new and speedier method, using Canadian mash ready mixed and supplied in large containers. Most of the stills were of modest size, ranging in capacity from ten to sixteen gallons. A much larger operation was carried on at the John Henry Camp farm near Cliff Haven, where corn meal kept two stills producing in wholesale quantities.

Moonshiners sold much of this product locally, usually to the night spots of Plattsburgh and surrounding towns. It was often high-powered stuff, could be sold for less per glass than smuggled goods, and to thirsty and undiscriminating customers was a satisfactory drink. Some of it, however, found its way along the "Rum Trail" to the south. It was occasionally promoted by the use of fake Canadian Club labels and bottles, a specialty of the still south of Plattsburgh.

Farmers could also grow more grapes that, if not of the best quality, were satisfactory for the making of wine. In 1921 the Internal Revenue Bureau announced that heads of families could make 200 gallons of wine a year for home use by obtaining a permit. A few county residents did so, but more of them made their own beer, supplementing the ingredients they could produce with others that were readily available. As long as they confined their production to amounts that they could consume at home, they were not likely to be molested. Only when they started to sell or transport it, as many of them did, were they liable to raids. Any purchaser who retailed home brew in his speakeasy was subject to prosecution regardless of how vile the stuff tasted, provided that it had more than one-half of one percent alcoholic content. Near beer was a product that just managed to keep within the law.

Crude corn whiskey could also be produced with a primitive apparatus, and if it was produced quietly and consumed at home it was not likely to attract the attention of enforcement officers. Clinton County never seems to have experienced the difficulty of Ogdensburg, where kitchen distillers caused flooded cellars from the quantity of corn and rye that they poured into the sewers.

Pharmacists were also directly involved with Prohibition because they could sell liquor prescribed by a doctor for medicinal purposes. Both pharmacist and doctor had to have a federal permit, but for a time the provisions of the Volstead Act were not enforced against the doctors. During the first four months of Prohibition 500,000 prescriptions were issued by Chicago's 3,000 doctors, of which 300,000 turned out to be spurious. One bed-ridden doctor issued 200 in the first two days, and he listed many strange complaints as requiring alcoholoc treatment. A degree of order was gradually brought into a confused situation as doctors were held to the letter of the law and brought into court by the hundreds for violation of the Volstead Act. New York's Mullan-Gage law between 1921 and 1923 permitted prescriptions for no more than one pint at a time and not more than one refill.

Briefly, in 1921 prescriptions for medicinal beer were legal, but the Congressional Willis-Campbell Act ended the practice. The law was upheld by the Supreme Court in 1924, to the relief of most druggists who regarded beer as bulky, probably unprofitable, and likely to drive other customers away. This left vinous and spiritous liquors that could still be prescribed; moreover, no law restricted the sale of patent medicines containing as much as sixty percent alcohol.

As early as 1922 the American Medical Association, which had favored national Prohibition, demanded the repeal of the medicinal parts of the Volstead Act. It cited the elderly patients who needed more whiskey than the law allowed, the invasion of the privacy of a doctor-patient relationship, and the current high prices that state control would reduce.

In 1931 the state almost acceded to the doctors' urgings. The legislature enacted the Hastings Bill which would have relaxed the restrictions on prescriptions and put the administration of the law in a division of the State Education Department. At a public hearing the Board of Regents and others voiced their opposition, and it was vetoed by Governor Roosevelt. Consequently, no change was made during the Prohibition years in New York State. In the prescribing and sale of medicinal beverages, however, North Country doctors and pharmacists kept sufficiently within the law to escape the kind of investigation and scandal that rocked other areas of the state and nation.

A Case Goes to Court

At a session of district court in Syracuse, 140 cases were on the docket. All of them were disposed of in one day, although the presiding judge, Harlan Howe, mistook a narcotics peddlar for just another saloon operator and fined him $100 instead of sending him to the penitentiary.

Jeremiah Davern of Plattsburgh

O NE DAY Officer Thwaits stopped a Pierce Arrow containing two couples. He discovered a case of Gordon's gin on the floor of the back seat. The driver was John R. Dunlap of New York City, and he and his passengers proved argumentative. When Thwaits asked questions he was told, "It's none of your goddam business." He rode with them to the trooper station in Au Sable Forks where Dunlap bellowed, "I'm getting pretty sick of this; get out!" At the station much more liquor was found, and the car and its passengers were taken to Plattsburgh for arraignment. There Dunlap tried to tell off the commissioner, who sent them all to the sheriff as "boarders" while they cooled off, with bail at $2,000 per person. A telephone call to New York, however, brought friends with the $8,000, and they were released pending trial.

Confiscation of liquor led to a court case only when people were arrested and charged with violating the law. Consequently, many seizures along the border

141

and roads of northern New York never reached court at all. This was true of most of the seizures on freight trains, where no one accompanied the consignment. It was also true of train passengers when smugglers could avoid being identified with the goods as well as the seizures of boats and cars whose owners successfully evaded capture. Great quantities of liquor were confiscated and destroyed for which no individual paid any penalty.

An elementary judicial procedure often occurred at the border. Noncommercial smugglers of a few bottles for personal use, if detected, signed an "offer of civil settlement" and paid a fine, but they were not arrested. Otherwise the courts would have been swamped with petty cases. Border officers had to decide when the contraband was sufficient in quantity to constitute commercial smuggling. An otherwise orderly person with only a few bottles could usually expect lenient treatment. In any case, border officers exercised in a small way the powers of a judge.

During the two-year life of New York's dry law the power to search, seize, and arrest was exercised by State Police, county sheriff, and Plattsburgh city police. If they made an arrest within the city, the suspect was tried in city court. Suspects elsewhere in the county went to county court. Until the repeal of the Mullan-Gage Act, searches and arrests could be made by state officers without a warrant. Very often violators of the Prohibition law were also found to be breaking state laws on gambling devices or disorderly houses. An average fine for possessing a slot machine was $25; other fines were supposed to fit the crime.

Throughout the Prohibition years the basis of

enforcement was the Volstead Act. Federal officers in the border service could make many kinds of searches and arrests without a warrant. To make an arrest an officer only had to believe that a law had been violated and that the person he was arresting had something to do with it. But warrants raised a host of legal problems. Federal officers had the right to search cars, luggage, barns, and sheds, but they had to have a warrant to search a person on the street or to enter some types of buildings, including private dwellings. A warrant could be obtained from court and it had to be based on evidence of lawbreaking and include a description of the specific property to be searched. Evidence to justify a warrant was obtained from complaints or from eyewitness accounts of officers. A common procedure was for an officer to buy an illegal drink; after obtaining a warrant, he returned to raid the place.

In the excitement of a pursuit or the eagerness to raid quickly where liquor was suspected, the legal technicalities were sometimes overlooked. Bootleggers were often able to regain their freedom and their cars because of faulty or missing warrants. Jeremiah Davern of Plattsburgh, who defended many bootleggers in court, won numerous acquittals when warrants were the main issue. For example, two bootleggers drove into a farmer's yard, stored their loaded car, and hired rooms for the night. They were raided, arrested, and their car impounded. They won their freedom and got their car back because the search was illegal without a warrant. Another case followed a raid on "Muskrat" Robare's still near Keeseville. Robare himself was convicted because he admitted ownership to save his father from arrest, but four other men were acquitted because the search had been made without a warrant.

Customs Officer Thwaits tells of a raid that was prevented altogether because of a faulty warrant. The Sunrise Hotel west of Plattsburgh dispensed liquor and also had a large shed which served as a transfer point. A friend of Thwaits bought six bottles of beer there, and on the strength of it Thwaits obtained a search warrant from the commissioner in Plattsburgh and with several troopers went to search the place. Thwaits believes that the proprietor had been tipped off by someone in the commissioner's office, because he challenged the warrant without seeing it, declaring that it lacked the proper description of the property. The authorities had ten days to get another warrant, which they obtained in Malone, but by that time the shed at the hotel had been cleaned out.

The courts sometimes made rulings that seemed to enforcement officers like setbacks to their work. In 1922 State Supreme Court Justice Angell ordered seventy cases of liquor returned to their Plattsburgh owner because of a defective search warrant. The complaint on which the warrant was based said only that the complainant had seen liquor taken to and from the premises; he had failed to say that it was spiritous or intoxicating, or that a sale had ever been made on the premises. In 1924 Federal District Judge Cooper ruled that a pilot car could not be seized. This vehicle was used not only to warn the caravan behind it of a trap ahead but also to frustrate a pursuit in every possible way. The judge ruled, however, that a pilot car contained no liquor, and that in any case conspiracy was

144

difficult to prove between the driver of the pilot car and the drivers of the loaded cars behind him.

But Judge Cooper himself got into trouble over warrants. A series that he issued resulted in massive raids and arrests between Albany and Canada in 1925. The raids were preceded by careful planning on the part of R. W. Merrick, prohibition chief in northern New York. Preparations included actual rumrunning between Canada and Albany by federal agents in order to gather evidence against the bootleggers. Cooper promised Merrick that if any of his agents were caught they would be released in their own cognizance so as not to expose them and put an end to their usefulness. When word of this arrangement leaked out, Cooper's impeachment was demanded by New York's Congressmen Emanuel Celler and Fiorello LaGuardia, who charged him with conspiring with Merrick to "entrap" bootleggers unlawfully. Called before the House Judiciary Committee, Cooper made a good appearance when he candidly explained what had happened and when he said that Prohibition, like any other statute, had to be enforced and "should not be made the subject of mockery and derision." The committee voted against impeachment 16–6, but members let it be known that all judges should view the hearing as a warning.

The Federal Supreme Court also made rulings that affected the enforcement of the law. One overruled lower federal courts on the conviction of two bootleggers who had been searched and arrested at the border by State Police several years after the repeal of New York's enforcement law. Previously, troopers had always been considered agents of the federal government, but according to Justice Brandeis, state officers who cooperated in enforcing the federal law were bound by the provisions of the Volstead Act which, except for federal officers, required warrants before search and seizure. This ruling was a blow to dry enforcement in those states like New York which had no enforcement code of their own. Henceforth the State Police must either cease much of their border activity or else be accompanied by a federal officer.

The Supreme Court additionally ruled that wiretapped evidence was admissible in a Prohibition case because it did not constitute search and seizure within the meaning of the Fourth Amendment. It separately declared that owners of autos seized in illegal activities might recover the vehicles if they were used without the owner's authorization. It also decided that lien-holders had a right to recover cars seized while they were being used in illegal activities. Both of these decisions unleashed much litigation over the ownership of bootleg vehicles. The Court further declared that a purchaser of intoxicating beverages was not guilty of violating the Prohibition laws and that Congress had "deliberately and designedly" omitted to impose a liability on the purchaser.

When he made an arrest, a border officer instituted a case that he was supposed to follow all the way through federal court. His first stop with his prisoner was the office of the United States commissioner in Plattsburgh. The commissioners during the Prohibition era were successively Henry Gilliland, William Pattison, and George Bixby, all distinguished citizens of the North Country. The commissioner held a preliminary hearing at which he heard both the officer's story and that of the arrested man, if he chose to tell it. The commissioner had to decide whether, first, a crime had been committed and second, the prisoner had had anything to do with it. If he decided that indeed a crime had been committed and the prisoner was involved he could order the prisoner to jail under bail and bind him over for a session of federal court.

In the early years, when a violation of the Volstead Act was only a misdemeanor, bail was typically set at $1,000. As violations became more flagrant, and especially after Congress made them felonies, bail started at $2,000, and its upper limits depended upon the seriousness of the charge and the number of previous offenses. Most prisoners spent little if any time in jail at this stage, bail usually being obtainable by a telephone call to their home towns. Bail was produced on the spot occasionally, almost as if the smuggler had prepared for a possibly expensive trip, but those who remained in jail at Plattsburgh for lack of bail were taken to court by the United States deputy marshal.

The job of the commissioner was not an enviable one, considering the unpopularity of Prohibition and the complexities of some of the cases that reached him. In 1929 Albert and Edward Doyle, boys from Whitehall, were brought to George Bixby's office. Albert was accused of transporting 381 quarts of Molson's ale, Edward of 351 quarts. The younger of the two was astonished at his $2,000 bail. Commissioner Bixby asked him if he knew he had made himself liable to five years in a federal prison and a $10,000 fine. "My God, no!" was the answer, as tears came to his eyes. His somewhat hardened older brother, Edward, smoked and hummed as he watched the proceedings. "Guess I'll have to go back into the game again to raise that," he remarked. Albert asked if he would have to stay in jail if he could not raise bail, to which the commissioner said yes. Edward turned his head toward Albert with a look of disdain for his weakness. Both boys were remanded to jail.

The *Plattsburgh Republican* in 1927 gave a tongue-in-cheek account of a day in the life of Commissioner Bixby.

Bixby entertained a family gathering in his office yesterday and a large attendance was reported. George Schule and party of Hawthorne, N.J. were the first guests to arrive. They were escorted by John P. Ross, deputy collector of customs, after the discovery of 34 bottles of whiskey in Schule's Chrysler sedan. Schule was held in $3,000 bail, but the rest of his party left early.

The party was just getting interesting when James Clark and party of five from Newark, N.J. put in their appearance attended by Lloyd D. Grace, deputy collector of customs. Clark very carelessly stopped at Rouses Point with a mixed assortment of liquor stowed away in a special compartment. Having contributed so much towards making the party a success, Clark was urged to stay and bail was fixed at $2,000.

Things were getting dead and someone had just suggested running over to the Meridian when Mr. and Mrs. Harold R. Herring of Weehawken, N.J., accompanied by Ernest Boller of North Bergen, N.J., blew in under the chaperonage of John D. Nicholson and Bert Fiske, deputy collectors of customs. They had had some difficulty finding their way to the party until they ran into the wines and liquors in the beautiful LaSalle sedan and immediately insisted upon the party joining the family gathering at Commissioner Bixby's office. They all proved such good entertainers that they were made permanent additions to the party, the two men held in $2,000 bail each and the woman in $1,000 bail. The gathering broke up at a late hour yesterday afternoon.

One of the commissioner's biggest "parties" followed the concerted raids of 1925. Judge Cooper had issued forty search warrants for Clinton County alone, and the arrests included all the big bootleggers of the area. They were arraigned before Commissioner Pattison, who fixed bail of $10,000 each for a long list of local professionals that included such names as Toissant Trombley, the Holland brothers, and Barney Duken.

When the commissioner bound a suspect over for trial, the case went to federal district court. The northern district of New York included twenty-nine counties in the central and northern parts of the state. Court was held several times a year, usually in Syracuse or Albany but occasionally in Binghampton or Auburn. Rarely was it held in Malone, and only once in Plattsburgh, perhaps because of the difficulty of impanelling a jury sympathetic to Prohibition in the counties on the Canadian border.

The judge who heard most of the Prohibition cases was Frank Cooper. A good lawyer, he was tough on violators, and rumrunners dreaded to appear in his court. He upheld the law rigorously and although not entirely sure about the wisdom of the Volstead Act, he had a Prohibitionist wife who perhaps stiffened his resolution. Judge Frederick H. Bryant of Malone also conducted sessions of court; he fell somewhat short of Cooper in the severity of his sentences. When Cooper was ill he was occasionally replaced by Harlan B. Howe of Vermont, who was more sympathetic to the bootleggers and whose penalties were relatively light.

The career of Jeremiah W. Davern illustrates the government's difficulty in getting and keeping good prosecutors. Davern became an assistant district attorney in 1917 and was thus a veteran when Prohibition cases began to appear. He personally typed out the indictments. On court day he presented cases to the grand jury on the second floor of the Syracuse courthouse, in between trying cases for the government on the floor below. All of these duties left him little time to practice law in Plattsburgh. For his services the government paid him $150 a month and four dollars a day for expenses which, when he paid two dollars for a room, left him only two dollars for meals. When he saw private lawyers receiving $100–150 for a five-minute speech, he resigned his federal job and spent his full time in a law practice in Plattsburgh which included numerous Prohibition cases. Yet he never lost the confidence of the federal judges, who realized his integrity in court.

Davern established a solid reputation which brought him cases from all over the state, often referred to him by lawyers in New York City. Out of appreciation for his efforts, his clients sometimes slipped him a bottle of good whiskey which had somehow found its way into their possession. As he explains it, "Now there were other lawyers that had these cases, but it got so that every serious case, a fellow had a bad case, it was in my office." One of these cases involved the daughter of a customs officer in New York. While visiting in Plattsburgh she accepted an invitation to spend an evening in Canada with a young man. When she discovered that he was smuggling beer on the return trip, she tried to persuade him to let her out of the car. Officers stopped his car en route, but the driver managed to escape, leaving the girl and the incriminating goods behind. Davern received the case by telephone from New York, and he convinced the federal court that she was not guilty of breaking the law. He helped his cause along because the judge occasionally had to leave the courtroom, "so this gave me practically two shots at the jury to tell my side of the story," says Davern.

The crucial testimony at court was offered by the patrolman who had made the arrest in the first place. If he failed to appear when the case was scheduled, it was usually dropped. Consequently, he sometimes had to spend several days in the city where court was being held. It was his job to tell the facts about the arrest, and the job of the defense attorney to discredit his testimony. Philip Auer recalls that John Judge, a Plattsburgh attorney, used to give him a hard time by trying to confuse him, but that Davern was "on the up and up." Other Plattsburgh lawyers who defended Prohibition clients were Robert Long, Edward Downs, and B. Loyal O'Connell. Patrolmen rarely tried to outwit the lawyers but stuck to a straightforward presentation of the facts, which was usually sufficient to assure conviction.

Most North Country lawyers and customs officers, as well as the accused, felt that trials at distant points all over the state were unfair and inconvenient. Lawyers had to be absent from their offices for two or three days per case, allowing for travel time. Border officers were sometimes absent for several days at a time, and the border was to a degree unpatrolled. In addition, as Robert C. Booth of Plattsburgh points out, federal juries were hand-picked, blue-ribbon panels which rarely reflected the ordinary man's feelings about the Prohibition law.

At federal court the first step was indictment by a federal grand jury. Failure to indict meant that the prisoner was freed from jail or bail, and the case was terminated. Indictment gave the accused the choices of pleading guilty or not guilty, and of demanding a jury trial. Cases in federal court, however, rarely went to a jury. The person charged, because of the tangible evidence against him, usually preferred a guilty plea to the risk of sentencing after a jury trial. The extent of his punishment was normally negotiated between the defense attorney and the federal district attorney. The presiding judge would usually concur in any agreement these two could reach.

This avoidance of trial helped federal courts cope with the mounting number of Prohibition cases. On one notorious day Judge Howe disposed of 140 of them; however, in the rush he absent-mindedly fined a narcotics peddlar as if he had merely sold beer, Davern recalls. One hundred cases a day were not unusual in many courts, and the Cooper court seems to have kept abreast of its work as well as any other. But as Prohibition cases alone grew nationally to 75,000 a year, serious congestion and overwork appeared in many district courts, despite quick convictions based upon guilty pleas; in any case this procedure was dubbed "bargain days," and it compromised the prestige of the courts everywhere.

The Volstead Act defined Prohibition violations as misdemeanors and provided penalties for first offenses of fines up to $1,000 or prison sentences up to six months. For second and subsequent offenses the fine was not less than $200 nor more than $2,000, and imprisonment for one month to five years. Yet the Syracuse court in April 1920 issued fines as low as $25, while the highest was $100. From the start Judge Cooper was stricter than most of his colleagues, and his severity gathered momentum as the decade progressed. By 1921 his fines for first offenders ranged from $150–750, exclusive of the loss of smuggled goods and cars. For a third offense one man received ten months at hard labor and a $1,500 fine. By 1923 Cooper was giving fines of $2,000–5,000, sometimes with prison terms attached. One woman was fined $500 even after her sad tale of being forced to break the law in order to support her four children. Not all the fines were paid, because some smugglers chose instead to sign the poor man's oath and serve thirty days in jail.

The court of the Northern Judicial District of New York, over which Cooper and Bryant presided, assessed fines of $448,747 in the fiscal year ending June 30, 1923. Only one judicial district in the country, the Northern District of California, exceeded this amount. But in fiscal 1924 the New York fines more than doubled, to $938,350, ninety percent of them for Volstead violations. Cooper believed that only severity would make the act work. His attitude, according

153

to Edward Schaffer, supervisor of the prohibition office in Albany, "causes the average bootlegger to hesitate before taking a chance in the northern district, or where they will come under the jurisdiction of Judge Cooper."

In 1924 and 1925, as repeaters increasingly appeared before him, Cooper stepped up his sentences. A Fort Covington man was fined $11,000 and sent to Atlanta for two years. Two Ticonderoga men were each fined $2,000 and sentenced to Atlanta for more than three years. A notorious Plattsburgh bootlegger, "Kid" Keene, was fined $2,000 and sent to Atlanta for four years. The last three sentences resulted from Cooper's drastic new plan of combining conspiracy and smuggling charges for violations of the tariff and customs laws together with the Volstead Act. Violations under the latter, being misdemeanors, were punishable only by fines and short jail sentences, but conspiracy, smuggling, and the possession of smuggled goods were felonies for which heavy fines and long prison sentences could be imposed.

Youthful offenders also appeared in court in growing numbers. Judge Bryant was bothered by them. They often did not know the name of their employer but had been promised big money and so had agreed to drive loaded cars and take all the risks, while the ringleaders went free. Bryant's fines were consequently light, but Cooper sent a seventeen-year-old high-school boy from Bombay to jail for three months on the occasion of his fourth arrest. During one trial he warned the youths "up around Plattsburgh" that they must not go to Canada and bring back liquor. If they persisted in doing it anyway, the judge declared, "It is false sentiment to let north country boys off easy when caught transporting liquor, for then others are not sufficently warned to keep out of the business." His sentences for youths were therefore comparable to those for older offenders.

In 1929 Cooper estimated that his efforts had already enriched the government by $5 million. Despite mounting evidence to the contrary, he continued to believe that swift and stern justice was the answer to liquor violations, and that a deep bite in the pocketbook was more effective than a short jail term. He probably reached these conclusions after viewing the number of repeaters who passed through his court and realizing that violators who went to prison were usually released before the expiration of their sentences and returned to bootlegging while still on parole. Hence his belief in the efficacy of heavy fines.

The Jones Act of 1929, which made violations a felony, provided maximum penalties for first offenders of $10,000 or five years *or both*. Yet for the fiscal year 1930 fines nationally averaged only $130, while prison sentences averaged 140 days. The federal court in New York City, which handed out fines of $5–10 under the Volstead Act, assessed $25–50 under the Jones Act in exchange for guilty pleas. On October 9, 1930, a total of 144 cases was processed with an average fine of $25. In April 1931, cases to the number of 2,700, a near record, were heard quickly and fines were light. Then the "bargain days" ended in New York City when U.S. Attorney George Z. Medalie persuaded the federal judges that the courts were being cheapened by this method of dispensing justice. Afterward fines averaged between $100 and $250, still only a small fraction of the legal limits.

Considering the volume of cases produced by Prohibition, perhaps the courts chose the only possible course of keeping up with their overcrowded dockets. The system at least resulted in a high percentage of convictions even if the sentences were low. In 1922 the *state* courts outside New York City handed down 3,900 Prohibition indictments, which resulted in 2,840 convictions, with many cases pending at the end of the year. These courts fined 2,259 people a total of $314,650, an average of $139, and sent 141 to jail for an average of 47 days. This took place when the state's Prohibition law was in force. In the *federal* courts outside New York City during the same year, 3,093 persons were indicted and 2,172 convicted, with many cases also pending at the end of the year. Fines were given to 1,898 persons, totalling $365,458 and averaging $193. Prison terms were given to 240, for an average of 22 days. In other words, while fining somewhat more heavily, federal courts were far more lenient than state courts in handing out jail sentences. Perhaps the most revealing fact, however, is the total of 7,000 Prohibition indictments in the courts of upstate New York during 1922.

By 1931 Prohibition arrests in New York averaged nearly 1,400 a month. Those who were convicted received fines averaging $57.90 or, if jailed, sentences averaging 108 days. In 1931, at the end of eleven years of Prohibition, 681,342 persons had been arrested nationally. Sentences were low but the rate of conviction had reached 85 percent. And still the country was flooded with illegal liquor!

The passage of a law is merely a beginning. Its enforcement depends in part upon the zeal of the officials, from patrolmen to members of the Supreme Court. Yet in the long run, enforcement depends upon the support, or at least the acquiescence of the people, and the Prohibition law did not achieve this. As violations mounted in numbers and violence the entire legal structure of the country was undermined. Clearly, modifications in the law or far more vigorous efforts to enforce it were in order. Americans chose the former course.

The End of an Experiment

Four and twenty Yankees,
Feeling mighty dry,
Took a trip to Canada
And bought a case of rye.
When the case was opened
The Yanks began to sing—
"To hell with the President!
God save the King!"

T HAT THIS VERSE found its way into the *Congressional Record* is some indication of the contemporary cynicism concerning the liquor traffic and Prohibition in general. When the *Literary Digest* reported after its 1930 poll that rural New York had gone wet, it was merely affirming what many of the citizens had suspected all along. Out of 638 ballots in Clinton County 299 favored the repeal of Prohibition, 250 wanted modification, and only 89 believed in enforcement of the existing laws. Of the five million polled nationally, 40 percent wanted repeal, 29 percent modification, and 31 percent enforcement. The poll was undoubtedly biased in favor of the wets; based upon owners of automobiles and telephones, it overemphasized the male voters, and it failed to persuade many drys to participate at all. Yet in the absence of a more balanced expression of opinion, the results were generally accepted as reflecting a trend.

This decisive shift in public opinion coincided with the great Depression. So did the administration of President Hoover. The first president willing to undertake serious law enforcement took office, ironically, when more and more people were becoming disillusioned with Prohibition. If governmental actions could have checked this deterioration, Hoover's should have done so. He conducted a dry campaign in 1928, and as president he left no doubt that he really wanted the law enforced.

His director of the Prohibition Enforcement Bureau, Amos W. W. Woodcock, started on the job with a major drive for enforcement and better relations with the states. Woodcock and the president were armed with the new Jones Act, which made felonies out of violations. The number of violators who went to jail doubled between 1929 and 1932, and the president began constructing six new federal prisons to relieve the overcrowding.

Whatever this activity might have accomplished earlier in the decade, it failed to reverse the drift of public opinion. Too many people had despaired of Prohibition, and too many channels for its violation had been opened. It was President Hoover's tragedy that the country turned its back on his dry thinking as it also repudiated his Depression leadership. Yet the Congress remained overwhelmingly dry until 1930; the Jones Act swept through the Senate in 1929 by a vote of 65-18, and the House by 284-90.

The vote on the Jones Act, however, represented the crest of the Prohibition wave in Congress. The election of 1930 increased the number of Democrats in the Senate and gave them control of the

House. This represented a substantial increase in the number of wets, although the drys were still firmly in control of both chambers; anyway, the campaign was fought over the Depression and the Republican failure to curb it, not over Prohibition.

The machinery of state governments meanwhile was being geared up for modification or repeal, and New York was one of the pace-setters. Having repealed its own enforcement act in 1923, it thereafter joined the ranks of wet states. Governor Smith publicly urged Congress to allow the states to define intoxicating beverages for themselves. He promised that if this were done he would tighten New York's laws against the saloon and hard liquor. He personally favored light wines and beer of 2.75 percent alcohol, and he accused Republicans of agreeing with him but not daring to say so. He became the wet candidate for the presidency in 1928, but the country was not yet ready for a change of party at the top. He was succeeded in the governorship by Franklin D. Roosevelt, no less wet than Smith but more cautious in expressing his ideas. He threatened at the outset, however, to veto any new enforcement bill that reached his desk.

Every session of the state legislature was characterized by determined dry efforts to reinstate Mullan-Gage or something like it. But sentiment in New York moved steadily in the opposite direction, and the same legislature that repealed the act in 1923 called for Congress to modify the Volstead Act by legalizing light wines and beers. It petitioned in 1926 for the states to be allowed to define intoxicating liquor.

In the fall of the same year the state ballot included a referendum on modifying the Volstead Act in favor of light wines and beer, a poll which Governor Smith called merely an expression of opinion. But, he added, "no public question in the last twenty-five years has caused as much conflict of public opinion as has this whole subject," and he reminded the voters that the legislature had ratified the Eighteenth Amendment seven years previously without first consulting them, as he had urged. The referendum carried by a 4–1 majority. New York City approved wine and beer by 7–1, and even rural Clinton County voted 5–3 in favor of the proposition. In the same election six other states voted wet on similar propositions. Together with New York, they contained one-fourth of the population of the country.

The next session of the New York legislature sent two resolutions to Congress. One called for modification of the Volstead Act along the lines proposed in the referendum; the other demanded an end to the government's poisoning of industrial alcohol. Governor Smith began to call for liquor control patterned after the Quebec system, that is, state monopoly of the liquor industry within its borders.

By 1931 the legislators had shifted from demands for modification to outright repeal. Despite Governor Roosevelt's wish not to be presented with wet bills which might compromise his presidential chances, the legislature considered five bills and three resolutions which attacked Prohibition in one way or another. Not all of them reached the Governor's desk. Of those that did he signed the Culliver Bill, which asked Congress to call a constitutional convention to consider repeal. Such a petition, however, could achieve its goal only when the legislatures of two-thirds of the states similarly asked Congress to call a convention. New Yorkers could see no other channels they could pursue to bring about changes on the national level.

Many respected New Yorkers joined the public debate. Nicholas Murray Butler, president of Columbia University and elder statesman of the Republican party, called for liquor control on the Quebec pattern. Representative Fiorello LaGuardia, later mayor of New York City, bitterly attacked Prohibition and satirized its extremes, pointing out that $200 million a year would be required to create some semblance of enforcement. United States District Attorney Emery Buckner of New York believed that enforcement in New York State would require more courts and $15 million a year at a time when Congress was providing only two-thirds of that amount for the entire country. Seymour Lowman, who succeeded to the command of the national enforcement machinery in 1927, echoed Buckner's sentiments by declaring that enforcement in New York alone would need 30,000 agents instead of the existing 300, and a score of new federal courts.

The Prohibition years spawned numerous organizations dedicated at first to modification and ultimately to repeal of the law. Yet their efforts at the beginning seemed puny compared to the great strength and respectability of the Anti-Saloon League and the WCTU. The first important one, the Association Against the Prohibition Amendment (AAPA) was founded in 1918, before the Eighteenth Amendment had even been ratified. It was followed by the Crusaders, made up of young businessmen who campaigned for "real temperance" instead of "prohibition temperance." The National Association Opposed to Prohibition brought hotel and real estate interests together, the Moderation League wanted a "reasonable" definition of intoxicating beverages, and the Voluntary Committee of Lawyers rejected Prohibition on constitutional grounds. The Woman's Organization for National Prohibition Reform came into existence in 1929, and even the American Legion and the American Federation of Labor came out on the side of the wets.

Until about 1926 organizations that fought Prohibition seemed not to be making any large impact. But in that year the Du Ponts, formerly dry, moved into leadership of the Association Against the Prohibition Amendment and brought with them high-powered leaders of industry, commerce, and politics with unlimited funds for their program. Many of them blamed their own high taxes on the government's loss of revenue from the distilleries and breweries, which only repeal could correct. They stole the thunder and tactics of the Anti-Saloon League with vast publicity and lobbying activities.

The Woman's Organization for National Prohibition Reform gave women their first important vehicle through which to work for repeal, and by 1932 they claimed a million members. Sophisticated, socially elite, and many of them related to the leaders of the AAPA, they made the WCTU seem dowdy by comparison. Known as the "Sabine Women" for Mrs. Pauline Sabin, one of the founders, they were also savagely attacked as "scarlet women" or "Bacchantian maidens" for betraying their sex and the "experiment noble in motive." Grace Root, daughter-in-law of Elihu Root and one of the leaders, remembers capturing one audience when, faced with her first microphone, she ad-libbed, "This is the first time I've ever stood in front of a speakeasy." They gave style and great energy to their campaign and, with their male counterparts in the AAPA, were probably the most influential groups working against Prohibition.

All of these groups bombarded the public with statistics concerning increased drinking, corruption, and the collapse of respect for all laws. They emphasized the loss to the government of tax revenues from legal alcohol. With the onslaught of depression in 1929 they sought to blame Prohibition for unemployment and farmers' hard times. Their economic arguments were not always sound, but they were readily accepted by a stricken people seeking explanations for the Depression. The shift in sentiment caught even the wet leaders by surprise, for as late as 1931 they anticipated several more years of agitation before changes in the Constitution could be effected.

The success of the wets paralleled the declining influence of the organizations which were once the heart of the Prohibition movement. The drys gradually lost the support of the nation's newspapers, in which they once had had a sympathetic hearing. In 1927 they also lost Wayne B. Wheeler, the imposing figure who had directed the Anti-Saloon League for so many years. His successor was Bishop James Cannon, Jr., who soon ran afoul of both the law and his own church and dragged his movement down with him. Even the Wickersham Commission, appointed by President Hoover to study Prohibition and law-enforcement, was a great disappointment to them in its final report of 1931. Of its eleven members, one urged repeal while seven recommended modifications or revisions. The majority wanted to allow Congress to return the subject "in whole or in part to the States, or to adopt any system of effective control."

In the summer of 1932, after nearly three years of hard times, the two political parties held their nominating conventions. The Republicans met first and they were presented with a choice between a wet and a moist plank. They adopted the latter by a mere 60 percent margin and renominated President Hoover to run on it. The plank called for the resubmission of the Eighteenth Amendment to the states and promised that the federal government would protect the states that wished to remain dry.

A few days later the Democrats moved into the same convention hall. They met in a victorious frame of mind with a relative unanimity on the Prohibition issue. Their plank, adopted by a 9–2 majority, promised repeal of the Eighteenth Amendment, federal help for the dry states, and the immediate modification of the Volstead Act so as to legalize beer. With the nomination of the wet Franklin D. Roosevelt, the lines were clearly drawn for a campaign between repeal and resubmission of the Eighteenth Amendment.

Repeal alone would probably not have carried the elections for the Democrats, because the moist proposals of the Republicans offered the drys their last hope and the moderate wets a reasonable alternative. But the larger Depression issues clearly favored the Democrats, who gained control of the presidency and Congress by commanding majorities. Also as a result of the November balloting a total of sixteen states had now repealed their dry laws.

The holdover or "lame-duck" Congress that convened in December 1932 failed to agree on a beer bill. It did succeed, however, in sending a repeal amendment to the states. The Senate adopted it on February 16 by a 63-23 vote, and the House four days later by 289-121. The amendment would repeal the Eighteenth Amendment and outlaw the liquor traffic across dry state lines, and it was to be considered by specially-chosen state conventions. The arithmetic of ratification worried the wets because thirteen states could block it. Twelve states were considered dry, while twelve others were uncommitted. Yet ratification required the approval of all the uncommitted states. Among the wet states the race began for the distinction of being the first to ratify, and Michigan won that honor on April 12.

In New York bitter rivalry marked the selection of delegates to the ratifying convention. District delegates were the goal of the drys, a single slate of delegates-at-large the intent of the wets. The wets won the argument and put together a bipartisan slate for a special election on May 23, where they carried the day by an 8-1 margin. New York City voted for them 40-1, and even Clinton County approved 3-1. On June 27, the 150 delegates formally voted for repeal, and New York became the eighth state to ratify the Twenty-first Amendment. In the record time of nine and one-half months, thirty-six states adopted it, the vote of Utah on December 5 bringing Prohibition to an end.

Meanwhile President Roosevelt called a special session of the new Congress for March 9. Four days later, in a seventy-two-word message, he asked for action on beer, a proposal greeted with wild whoops and

167

cheers. Next day the House adopted 3.2 beer by a lopsided vote. It provided a five-dollar tax per barrel and $1,000 a year from each brewery. The bill was rushed to the Senate by special messenger, where it received more decorous treatment. On March 16 the Senate approved 3.05 beer. However, it accepted the conference report for 3.2 beer, the president signed the measure on March 22, and beer became legal on April 7 in twenty-two states.

Although New York's political leaders had been demanding beer for years, they now failed to agree on the regulatory machinery before the date that beer became legal. Governor Herbert H. Lehman's proposals got caught in a cross-fire of politics. One Republican assemblyman, Horace M. Stone, commented during the debate: "I feel he [Lehman] has been in office sufficiently long to acquire something of the propensities of his predecessors, Smith and Roosevelt, both of whom thought the Legislature was a sort of subordinate adjunct to the Executive Department." In other words the issue brought out not only Republican-Democratic animosities but legislative-executive rivalry as well.

The deadlock in Albany continued past the date that beer became legal. For several weeks beer was sold under local ordinances. In Plattsburgh the City Council held a special session on April 6, and adopted guidelines for the sale of beer within the city. All of the arrangements were considered temporary until the state assumed control, but meanwhile beer could be sold locally in drug stores, bona fide clubs, grocery stores, hotels, and restaurants. The first beer arrived in the city on April 11. Other communities in the state

168

allowed beer sales at gasoline stations, lunch wagons, road stands, and news rooms. Many localities, including Plattsburgh, undertook to close all the speakeasies in order, according to the local chief of police, to protect the legal beer sellers "but also to protect the consumers who are running a risk drinking the mixtures afforded by speakeasies." The zeal for enforcement, so often lacking under Prohibition, was notably present after repeal.

On April 7 the governor offered a compromise which the legislature adopted three days later. State control of the sale of beer was to go into effect on June 1. The 60,000 retail outlets legalized under local ordinances would be reduced by the denial of state licenses to thousands of roadside stands, news rooms, and candy and cigar stores.

And so New Yorkers and other Americans began to drink legal beer again. In New York licensees tried to avoid conflict with the new Alcoholic Beverage Control Board, which meant that among other actions they got rid of illegal slot machines. The advent of legal beer quickly put the smugglers out of business. Indeed, they were among the minority who genuinely mourned the passing of Prohibition. But for the most part border patrolmen, police, judges, and the general citizenry of the North Country breathed a sigh of relief over the end, they hoped, of lawlessness and violence.

But in many respects the old saloon was brought back to life, the only difference being that bars must be open to view. On the other hand, the Depression speakeasy was put out of business, partly from the difficulty of getting beer, and partly by the force of public opinion and the determined efforts of the local police. For many people the Democratic slogan "Happy days are here again" became literally and personally true. But for many others the haste and excesses of repeal removed all hope that Prohibition might be succeeded by moderation in the drinking habits of the nation.

Sources

FOR THE LOCAL SCENE extensive use has been made of the newspapers of northern New York, especially the *Plattsburgh Republican*. The files of the *New York Times* have been exceedingly helpful for both national and local coverage of the Prohibition era. A publication of the *Chateaugay Record* of Chateaugay, New York, "The Chateaugay Thaw and Bootlegging Tales," includes reminiscences of border residents.

Stimulating interpretations were found in such books as Andrew Sinclair's account of *Era of Excess, A Social History of the Prohibition Movement* (New York: Harper & Row, 1964) and Denis Tilden Lynch's *Criminals and Politicians* (New York: Macmillan, 1932).

Interviews have been conducted with the following people:

LAW ENFORCEMENT OFFICERS

Philip Auer of Plattsburgh
Ralph J. Chilton of Rouses Point

Walter Connelly of Rouses Point
Roy Delano of Rouses Point
Robert Halstead of Rouses Point
John Ross of Rouses Point
Henry Thwaits of Au Sable Forks,
    assisted in his paperwork by Mrs. Thwaits

ATTORNEYS

Robert C. Booth of Plattsburgh
Jeremiah Davern of Plattsburgh

BOOTLEGGERS

Leo and Diane Filion of Champlain
Gaston Monette of Rouses Point
Francis ("Sam") Racicot of Rouses Point

SPECTATORS

Fuller Allen of Plattsburgh
Mrs. Lavinia Bullis of Champlain
Elmer Caron of Champlain
Howard S. Curtis, formerly of Mooers
Darwin L. Keysor of Plattsburgh
Charles W. McLellan of Champlain
Ralph Sanger of Rand Hill, Beekmantown
Trefle Trombley of Champlain

RUM ACROSS THE BORDER

was composed in 11 on 13 Compugraphic Century Schoolbook,
by Metricomp;
with dust jacket display type set in Twogar Caps by Rochester/Monoheadliners;
printed on 55-pound, acid-free Glatfelter Antique Cream and
Notch bound with paper covers printed in 2 colors
by Maple-Vail Book Manufacturing Group, Inc.;
and published by

SYRACUSE UNIVERSITY PRESS
Syracuse, New York 13244-5160